The Archaeology of London
Series editors: John Schofield and Alan Vince

ROMAN LONDON

Dominic Perring

London

© Dominic Perring 1991
First Published 1991

Typeset by Setrite Typesetters, Hong Kong
and printed and bound in Great Britain
by Biddles Ltd., Guildford, England
for the publishers
B. A. Seaby Ltd.
7, Davies Street
London W1Y 1LL

Distributed by
B. T. Batsford Ltd.
P.O. Box 4, Braintree, Essex CM7 7QY

British Library Cataloguing in Publication Data
Perring, Dom
Roman London. — (The Archaeology of London).
1. London (City). Roman Empire antiquities. Excavation of remains
I. Title   II. Series
936.212

ISBN 1-85264-039-1

Contents

Preface and acknowledgements

Precious little of Roman London survives and the destruction of Roman levels continues fast as new office foundations are sunk ever deeper into ancient levels. In recent years the close attention of the archaeologists of the Museum of London, encouraged by the cooperation of City developers, has allowed the detailed recording of much that is being lost. In just four years, from 1986 to 1989, work was started on about 200 archaeological sites in the City, and many others were dug in the neighbouring boroughs. Every year a mountain of new information and material is added to the stores of the Museum of London. Far too many new data are coming in for them all to be studied properly, with much being stored against the day that time and money can be found to permit more leisurely analysis.

The first purpose of this book is to bring together as much as possible of this new information, in the hope that it will allow progress to be assessed and new questions asked. It is also written with certain specific problems in mind. Much of the fascination of Roman London derives from its history of extremes; it burst into life with extraordinary vigour and quickly became one of the largest cities in the Roman west but boom seems rapidly to have turned to bust. After a short period of readjustment, which saw a sharp decline in population, a new but very different Roman town spread over the ruins of the old. This town was in turn to fade and fail, leaving little behind but its walls and name. How could a city grow so fast, change so much and fall so far? These are the questions that this work attempts to address.

This book is necessarily a personal interpretation, one particular view of how London rose and fell, but it owes an enormous amount to the generous help of many friends and colleagues. My greatest debt is to Tim Williams, a constant source of advice and encouragement, and I owe very special thanks to David Bentley, Trevor Brigham, Frances Grew, John Shepherd and Brian Yule for having given so freely of their ideas and time. I am also most grateful to Nick Bateman, Gary Brown, Mark Burch, Sue Cole, Barbara Davies, Geoff Egan, Jenny Hall, Julian Hill, Cath Maloney, Dick Malt, Marie Nally, Beth Richardson, Sue Rivière, Peter Rowsome and R. S. O. Tomlin for keeping me up to date on recent discoveries and giving me access to unpublished work. Although less directly involved in the preparation of this book I have learnt much about the archaeology of Roman London from Patrick Allen, Charlotte Harding, John Maloney, Gustav Milne and Steve Roskams; and my very considerable debt to the work of Harvey Sheldon, Peter Marsden and Ralph Merrifield should be clear from the references in the text. There are very many others whose considerable contribution to the archaeology of London I am unable, for want of space, to acknowledge properly. In deference to the wishes of my past colleagues at the Museum of London I would like to emphasize that although this work is in many respects a product of their researches it was not sponsored by the Museum and should not be taken to represent the views of that organization; the author alone is to blame where facts or opinions have been misrepresented.

Alan Vince (a sympathetic and forbearing guardian editor), John Schofield and Tim Williams were kind enough to read carefully through earlier drafts of this work and have helped smooth out many of the rougher passages of text, moderate some of the wilder statements and correct various errors of fact. Paul Blockley prepared the new line drawings with customary skill and efficiency; and the photographic plates, which are reproduced by permission of the Board of the Museum of London (with the exception of Fig. 20 which is reproduced by kind permission of Mr Brian Philp), were prepared with the help of Jan Scrivener and Peter Hinton. Consent to reproduce Fig. 41 was generously given by Tom Blagg and Sheila Gibson.

My family have been quite remarkably patient in the months of my obsession with this project, and without the generosity of my parents-in-law, Giuseppina and Renato Merlo, I would not have found the time or peace to produce a completed text.

Introduction

Some comments on the nature of the ancient city

The Roman empire was an urban empire. Where Rome found no cities it was obliged to create them, and where cities could not survive then neither could Rome. The city was the basic administrative unit where the ruling élite could compete for office, judge disputes and govern, where taxes could be determined and defences organized. Cities were also sacred places since the affairs of government needed divine guidance, and communities were bound together by city festivals organized in honour of the gods.

The economic role of the city was less important. Land was the principal source of wealth, whether in the form of rents or agricultural surplus and Classical cities never escaped the domination of the agricultural landowners. The self-governing city and its surrounding territory, although clearly defined one from the other, were administratively indivisible (Finley 1973). Long-distance trade in the ancient world was principally concerned with the small-scale transfer of luxury items and precious materials. Trade in less valuable goods remained severely limited by the prohibitive cost of transport, and local self-sufficiency was the norm.

The rapid growth of the Roman empire had an important effect on urban trade. The profits of conquest and empire were vast and unevenly spread, and the leading citizens of Rome became very rich indeed. This wealth was naturally invested in land, and large slave-run estates grew up in many parts of Italy. The demand for slaves was considerable and stimulated a major trade, paid for in part by the export of wine and oil. The profits of empire were also directed towards the competition for status in the towns; theatres, temples and baths were built to enhance the prestige of the leading houses and incidentally created work in the towns. Large towns with large appetites could grow, and urban trade became more necessary and more profitable (Hopkins 1978).

Two institutions of Rome, paid for by the profits of empire, had a major influence on the development of towns and trade in the Roman provinces. One of these, the grain supply of Rome, was effectively confined to the Mediterranean provinces but the other, the Roman army, was of enormous importance in the north-west. Soldiers in the frontier provinces were comparatively rich and their spending power had a marked impact on local economies. Of even greater importance were the extended supply lines which linked the various military outposts. Army supply was rarely left to the vagaries of the market; goods were moved to order by private shippers who had won state contracts, and these men used state transport for their private profit when possible. As a consequence long-distance trade became parasitic on official supply lines, and in effect the state provided subsidized transport for goods travelling certain routes (Whittaker 1989, 71–2; Middleton 1979).

The period of imperial growth allowed trade to grow to unprecedented levels and those engaged in commerce during this period could make very considerable profits. Social attitudes, supported by legislation, limited the extent to which élites could involve themselves in trade but the extensive use of slaves, freedmen and other intermediaries allowed men of standing to participate indirectly (D'Arms 1981). On the frontiers power lay in the hands of military commanders rather than with the landed élite and here merchants may have been free of constraints found elsewhere. A few of the larger ports, such as Ostia, the main port of Rome, may also have been successful enough to have permitted the brief emergence of a 'middle class', and tolerated an unusual degree of social mobility (Meiggs 1973), but these places were exceptional. At the time of the conquest of Britain trade had become far more important to urban prosperity than had previously been the case but the foundations of urban society remained broadly unchanged.

When Roman armies landed in Britain in AD 43 the British had yet to develop an urban society of the type familiar to Rome. Once the glory of conquest and spoils of war had been won the principal concerns of Rome were to impose peace and taxes, objectives which could only be achieved with the help of the local élite. A governor was put in charge of the province, but he had only a small administrative staff. Outside military affairs the main duties of the governor were supervisory and adjudicatory, and it was expected that local administration, the responsibility for raising taxes and administering justice, would remain in the hands of the traditional élites. These owed loyalty to Rome since their position was enhanced as agents of the empire and protected by the *pax Romana*. Towns gave these élites common purpose and identity, and enabled them to enjoy the material and political benefits which derived from their favoured relationship with Rome. Conceptually the empire was less a single state than a federation of allies, a collection of self-governing city states which paid tribute to Rome in exchange for Roman protection. Where towns existed the colonial administration needed only to superimpose itself on the traditional political élites and make them dependent on it for their share of the accumulated surplus. Where they did not, as in Britain, conquest was necessarily followed by an active programme of urbanization.

The character of Roman London

Roman London was unlike any other settlement in the province of Britain, and indeed unlike most to be found elsewhere in the empire. Just as modern London is hardly representative of the contemporary English town so its Roman counterpart stood as something apart. It was undoubtedly the largest and arguably the most Roman city of Britain. For much of the period London was the principal point of contact between the imperial power and its frontier territory; this was the spot through which all British roads passed on their way to Rome. London's fortunes were to ebb and flow with the tide of imperial interest. London is important, therefore, not just as the principal town of Roman Britain but also as a town of the Roman empire; a mirror not of Rome but of its imperial vigour.

London is likely to have been a recognizably Roman town for about 350 years, perhaps a little longer, and its story is a complex one. Recent City excavations have made a priority of the study of evidence for change; small rescue sites may not favour the recovery of full building plans but they do allow the close study of all surviving traces of occupation, right down to earliest levels. Because hundreds of these small sites, dotted across the town, have now been examined we know far more about the changing face of Roman London than we do about the development of many better preserved cities. On each site the build-up of floors and walls, where new buildings had risen over the levelled remains of the old, has contributed to our understanding of the changing city. To allow comparison from one site to another, and to place the observed changes in some kind of historical context, dates are needed. Most archaeological excavations recover large quantities of pottery which, because styles changed, can be dated. Imported tablewares, especially the shiny red Samian ware made in Gaul, can be dated very closely indeed. Coins too are a valuable source of dates. There were periods, however, when new types of coin and pottery were scarce and old types remained long in use. Finds will in any case only suggest a date after which something had occurred; how much after is not always clear. For these reasons archaeological dates tend to be approximate rather than exact, and caution is required when comparing them with historical ones. For the Roman period this chronological imprecision is often glossed over by talking in terms of imperial eras. For the sake of narrative such terms are widely used in this book but it should be remembered that there is far more greyness at the edges of archaeological dating than they imply. 'Flavian' here means 'broadly the last third of the first century AD' rather than 'precisely AD 69−96' as it should.

There are a few instances, however, where greater precision can be achieved and 'real' dates suggested. We know from historical sources that London was burnt to the ground during the revolt led by Queen Boudicca

(Boadicea) in AD 60, and it is reasonable to assume that buildings burnt in the mid first century were destroyed at this time. Some inscriptions can be dated from internal evidence, such as references to emperors and governors, but London has produced few of these. Of far greater importance is tree-ring dating, or dendrochronology. Large timbers were widely used in London in the construction of the waterfront, as piles beneath stone foundations and to line wells and drains. In some instances these timbers have survived and they can be dated from their seasonal growth rings. Where the sapwood is preserved it is possible to be fairly precise about the years in which timbers were felled. When many timbers were used in a single construction buildings can be dated precisely. The techniques for dating the timbers of Roman London have only recently been perfected, but have already provided information which has radically altered our understanding of the city.

1 The birth of London (*c.* AD 50−60)

London before the Romans

Roman London was built on the north bank of the Thames, the site of the modern City. The river, roughly in its present position by the time of the Roman conquest, was probably tidal at London, although tides may not have reached as far as Westminster (Milne 1985, 79−86). At high tide the river may have been as much as 1 km across and most of the south bank would have been submerged, although there were important islands of dry land at Westminster and Southwark. At low tide the channel would have shrunk to about 275 m, still considerably wider than the river of today which is about 200 m across. On its north side the Thames had cut against a pair of low hills, and it was here that the town was built. The western hill, Ludgate Hill, is now occupied by St Paul's Cathedral whilst that to the east (hereinafter referred to as Cornhill) is presently surmounted by Leadenhall market. These hills were separated by the valley of the Walbrook, the upper parts of which remained marshland until reclaimed in the Roman period. To the west of Ludgate Hill was the Fleet river, and on both hills there were springs which fed small streams.

Despite intense search no trace has been found of any immediately pre-Roman occupation in the City, although several sites have produced remains of earlier prehistoric activity, especially in the area of Bishopsgate. The skeleton of a young man found at the Tower of London might have been buried in the late Iron Age but this is far from certain (Parnell 1985, 5−7). The distribution of certain pre-Roman coin types seems to indicate that some form of centre had been established in the lower Thames valley, west of London, in the early first century BC (Kent 1978, 53−8; Haselgrove 1988). There is no evidence, however, that this hypothetical site had continued beyond *c.* 60 BC and it is of little evident relevance to the later history of the area. We can be reasonably certain that there were no major settlements in or around London at the time of the conquest.

Limited pre-Roman occupation has been noted at both Westminster and Southwark, where the islands of dry ground next to the river had attracted settlement (Merriman 1987, 324). The most interesting evidence

FIG. 1 The grave of a woman buried in the mid first century AD, found in excavations at Harper Road, Southwark. The coffin was accompanied by grave-goods: a bronze neck-collar and mirror can be seen by the feet and a flagon by the head.

comes from Southwark. At 15–23 Southwark Street gullies sealed by early Roman buildings, and perhaps themselves associated with timber buildings, had contained Iron Age pottery (Beard and Cowan 1988, 376). The upper fills of one of the gullies contained the bronze fittings from a sheath for a Roman *dolabrum*, or military axe. Associated finds included a coin of 25 BC–AD 25. In excavations at 124 Borough High Street the burial of a young man was found beneath a layer containing conquest-period pottery (Goodburn 1978, 453). This was in turn cut by three parallel rows of post-pits, probably of post-conquest date, which were sealed by the first-century road to London Bridge. The burial of a woman, about 35 years old, found at Harper Road has been dated to the middle of the first century AD (Fig. 1). The body had been placed in a wooden coffin and was accompanied by a flagon, a bronze neck-collar and the remains of a square tinned bronze mirror which had probably been made in Italy (Dean and Hammerson 1980, 17–22). Late Iron Age coins and pottery have also been found on other sites in Southwark. The evidence seems to suggest occupation of both the later Iron Age and early Roman period, perhaps with no interruption between the two. It also seems probable that the Iron Age occupation consisted of no more than a few buildings, perhaps a farmstead. There was certainly no city here; London was a Roman creation.

The arrival of Rome

We know that the army crossed the Thames in AD 43 and Dio, a historian born over a century after the event, believed that this happened 'at a point where the river flows into the sea and at high tide forms a pool'. Since the object of the crossing was a march on Colchester the lowest crossing that seemed practicable would have been preferred; several sites from Westminster to Tilbury can be proposed (Fuentes 1985, 94; Huggins 1986, 195). We also know that at this point in the campaign the invasion forces awaited the arrival of the Emperor Claudius before advancing on Colchester, and it is reasonable to assume that a conquest-phase encampment was established somewhere near the Thames. It would in any case have made tactical sense to have arranged for the control of this strategic crossing. No early fort has yet been discovered and until we know more it is difficult to assess properly the influence of the presumed early military presence on the later development of the area.

Some evidence for the strategic importance of the site comes from the study of the Roman street system (Fig. 2). The Roman administration required direct links between the ports of the south-east and the areas of military deployment to north and west, and the roads which converged on the Thames were born of this need. The shortest Channel crossing

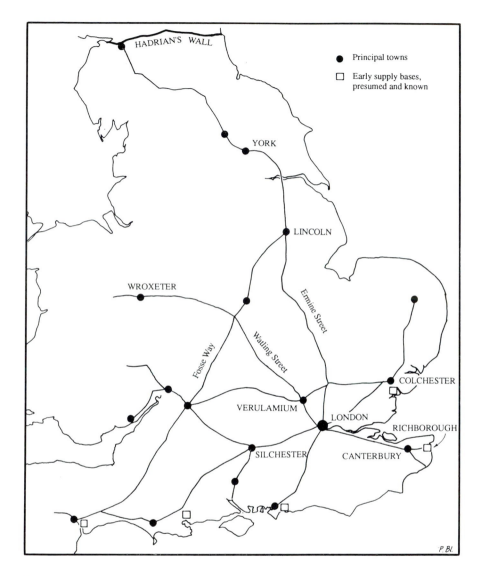

FIG. 2 A map of Roman Britain showing some of the principal sites mentioned in the text and illustrating the strategic position of the site of London.

dictated that the main landing sites and supply depots were near the Channel ports. Richborough was by far the most important. From here the main centres at Colchester and Verulamium (St Alban's), and forts at Wroxeter and Lincoln, could only be reached by crossing the Thames; the road and coastal links from Richborough to the Thames therefore formed the trunk of a communication system which branched once the Thames was crossed. The combined need to cross the river and bring supplies inland along the river suggested the site of London. The point where these various streets were brought together, where they crossed the Thames, was the hub of the provincial communication system (Margary 1967, 53).

The original crossing of the Thames may have been at Westminster not London. Watling Street, the Roman road from Kent to Verulamium, is likely to have followed a pre-Roman track and the line of the street, on both sides of the Thames, points towards the area of Westminster rather than the City (*see* Fig. 18) (Margary 1967, 54). The deviations in the line of Watling Street may, however, have been due to problems of terrain, and the projections of the known stretches of Watling Street do not actually meet at the Westminster ford (Esmonde-Cleary 1987, 117). Nor have any traces of a road through Westminster yet been found, even though excavations have been made at some appropriate points (Grew 1980, 381).

Excavations in Southwark have produced evidence of two major roads approaching the river bank (Fig. 3) (Graham and Hinton 1988). They were directed to a point, presumably the site of the Roman bridge (although this might arguably have been preceded by a ferry), near the modern London Bridge. The principal road was the Kent road, the continuation of Watling Street, and this had been laid over layers of logs forming causeways across the lower and muddier areas. Finds from layers associated with the earliest use of the road suggest that it should be dated *c.* AD 45–60. The second road was slightly narrower and crossed the centre of the island of dry ground, and it could have continued towards Westminster although this has yet to be established; this road may not have been laid until after AD 60. We therefore find that no roads leading to a conquest-phase (*c.* AD 43) crossing have yet been recognized, whilst the earliest approaches to London from Southwark may not have been established until slightly later. The evidence allows three interpretations: the roads leading through Southwark to London were part of a later revision to a Roman street system initially directed to a ford at Westminster; the roads in Southwark are slightly earlier than the evidence implies; or the Roman street system of south-east Britain is later than is generally assumed. It is not inconceivable that Rome continued to use pre-Roman routes for a few years after the conquest and that the roads in Southwark were therefore an original part of the Roman road system. Because of these uncertainties we do not yet know if London was planned integrally with the provincial road system, or whether it was an afterthought which the road-building authority (the army) was obliged to accommodate. If the former then London must have been conceived by the imperial administration, if the latter then its foundation might have owed more to traders and merchants able to recognize the commercial potential of the site.

The first Roman London

London is unlikely to have been earlier than the Thames crossing since the site was of little value if inaccessible from the south, and this could only be reached by the roads and causeways which crossed the mud-flats and tidal channels of Southwark (Fig. 3). Since these seem most likely to have been built *c.* AD 50–55 then this is the probable date for the first settlement of London. Coins found in excavations on both banks of the river provide the basis for this suggested dating. Most Claudian coins found in London were not from the official mints of Rome but were copies, forgeries really, produced to make up for the fact that there were too few 'real' coins around. Sites with a high proportion of official coins tend to date from the first period of conquest, whilst those with a higher proportion of the irregular issues were usually occupied later in the reign of Claudius, who ruled until AD 54. The proportion of irregular issues from Southwark, 91 per cent of all Claudian coins, is high, and the commonest types are most likely to have been struck *c.* AD 50–55 (Hammerson 1978a, 1988). Coins from excavations in the City present a similar picture. Peter Marsden writing in 1980 found that 87.5 per cent of Claudian coins were irregular issues (Marsden 1980, 28), whilst the figure for coins found in more recent excavations seems to be at least 80 per cent (according to provisional identifications made by Jenny Hall). The evidence suggests that there was a busy settlement of the late Claudian period where many coins were lost. It remains possible, however, that there had been an earlier but much smaller settlement where too few coins were lost to have had any effect on the overall statistics.

Evidence from excavations in the City allows it to be suggested that there had been a small Claudian establishment, of uncertain date but not necessarily earlier than AD 50, which had been considerably enlarged *c.* AD 55. A close study of the distribution of pre-Flavian pottery (earlier than *c.* AD 69) shows that the heart of the early town lay north of London Bridge, on the southern side of Cornhill; excavations near the junction of Lombard Street, Gracechurch Street and Fenchurch Street have produced proportionally more early pottery than sites elsewhere in the City. The first buildings in this part of London were set parallel or perpendicular to the river, and the absence of alignments at a diagonal suggests that the layout was ordered from the start (Williams in preparation). The only known exception to this was a timber structure, more like a shed than a house, found in excavations at 5–12 Fenchurch Street (Hammer 1985, 7–8). This building, possibly the earliest on the site, was set askew to the other structures in the area; perhaps because it was built before the town had been properly organized but more probably because it was set casually in an open plot. It has been claimed that in its earliest phase, *c.* AD 50–70, 'the settlement grew somewhat haphazardly at the junction of the road network and the navigable Thames' (Milne 1985, 149), but what we know of the arrangement of streets and buildings on Cornhill suggests order rather than chaos.

The principal and possibly earliest streets of London were those which formed a T-junction at its centre and linked the Thames crossing with the main routes east and west (Fig. 3). To the north of the road junction was a gravelled area at least 25 m across, perhaps a central square or piazza, where in later years the forum was built. Timber buildings, probably of Claudian date (earlier than *c.* AD 55), had been built alongside the main east−west road (Philp 1977, 7−9). Little is known of the character of the occupation at this time and archaeological opinion has been divided

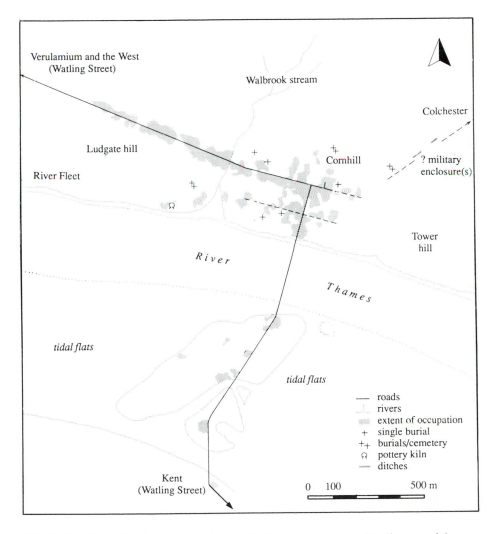

FIG. 3 Pre-Flavian London, showing the extent of occupation in *c.* AD 55. The core of the settlement, on Cornhill, was surrounded by early burial sites and ribbon development alongside approach roads.

between those who would rather see these buildings as part of a military establishment, a fort or supply base, and those who prefer to see London's origins as entirely civilian. These arguments will be considered further towards the end of this chapter.

Whether military or civilian, the site is likely to have been defined by recognizable boundaries. Roman forts were usually surrounded by impressive ramparts and ditches; city boundaries too were an important element of the ancient landscape, although sometimes marked by no more than boundary stones. The early boundaries of London were swept away in the later growth of the city but the distribution of burials, which were not allowed inside Roman towns, offers clues as to their location. Several early burials have been found surprisingly close to the centre of Roman London. Several pre-Flavian cremations were found in recent excavations at Leadenhall Court and another was found at 25−26 Lime Street (T. Brigham, personal communication; Williams in preparation). Single cremations have also been found at Bank underground railway station, near King William Street (Crooked Lane), beneath Lombard Street and at 12 Laurence Pountney (RCHM 1928, 155). Another may have been found in Nicholas Lane (although see Merrifield 1965, 276). Since single burials do sometimes crop up inside Roman towns, despite the rules to the contrary, this evidence must be treated with caution. It can also be argued that the pre-Flavian settlement at London had not always been considered urban, that for a period it had no formal boundaries and exercised no control over the disposal of its dead, but the available evidence suggests that the contrary was the case. The site seems to have been planned from the start, and it is possible that these burials were outside the earliest settlement. This first London might have been restricted to a small area on the Cornhill, perhaps about 200 m east−west by 300 m north−south. No remains of an early boundary around such an area have yet been recognized. There have been several excavations close to the borders of this proposed Claudian settlement but no major system of ditches and ramparts has been found; the site was probably not defended.

A defended site of the Claudian period might, instead, have been located some 300 m to the north-east of the area described above (Fig. 4). A ditch, considered likely to be a military feature on the basis of its characteristic V-shaped profile and early date, was first recognized on a site north of Aldgate and has since been recorded on two sites by Fenchurch Street (Chapman and Johnson 1973; Rivière and Thomas 1987; Heathcote 1989, 50). A total length of 130 m has been recorded. It was 1.8−2.4 m across and 1.3 m deep, with a square cleaning-trench at its base. Finds from the ditch fills are consistent with a Claudian date and included the bone handle-grip of a legionary sword; the fills of the ditch were covered by buildings which were probably destroyed in the fire of AD 60. This feature lay *c.* 20 m to the north of the Colchester road, and

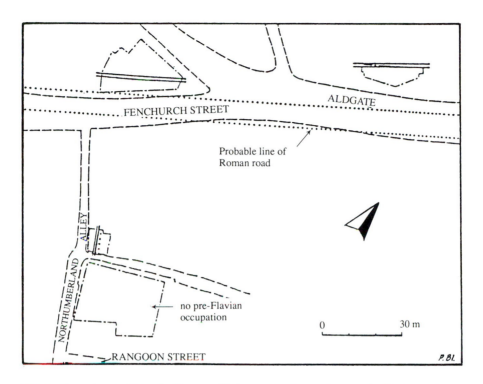

FENCHURCH STREET

ALDGATE

Probable line of
Roman road

no pre-Flavian
occupation

0   30 m

P.BL

FIG. 4 Plan of early ditches in the area of Aldgate (based on a drawing by Rivière and Thomas). It has been suggested that this was the site of a Claudian fort but the absence of evidence for early occupation at Rangoon Street puts this in doubt.

perhaps converged on its line, but it is not clear if road and ditch were contemporary; roadside buildings were destroyed in AD 60 but the street need not have been laid before *c.* AD 55. The ditch is more likely to have been contemporary with the first phase of occupation of London in *c.* AD 50, although an earlier date cannot be precluded.

A ditch of similar form and date, perpendicular to the Fenchurch Street ditch, was found some 60 m to the south at 9 Northumberland Alley; a row of pits to the east of the ditch may have supported a palisade. Excavations within the angle formed by the ditches have consistently failed to produce evidence for any internal buildings. Most of the sites in this area were small and their evidence cannot be given too much weight but this was not the case at Rangoon Street, to the south-east of Northumberland Avenue, where careful excavations over a large area failed to find any evidence for Claudian occupation (Bowler 1983). Either the proposed fort was left empty, had not extended this far to the south, or did not exist at all. If restricted to the area to the north of Rangoon Street the defended enclosure was less than 80 m wide; a small and strangely elongated fortlet rather than a fort. It is possible that the various ditches were not part of a military camp at all but had surrounded a number of different enclosures, paddocks and compounds, to either side of the road.

London's early growth

By the Boudiccan revolt a simple street grid had been laid out over the area of the earliest settlement on Cornhill (Fig. 5). There were at least three streets aligned east–west and another three north–south. One of the lesser north–south roads is likely to have been in place *c*. AD 55, a date suggested by recent excavations in Whittington Avenue where gravel road surfaces have been uncovered, and by work at 25–26 Lime Street where part of the roadside ditch was excavated (G. Brown, personal communication; Williams in preparation). Finds beneath another of these roads, at 19–21 Birchin Lane, indicate that this was no earlier than *c*. AD 55 and that it had been built or widened after the area had already been occupied for some years; adjacent buildings show that this road was probably in place by the time of the Boudiccan revolt in AD 60 (Marsden 1987, 79–82). The earliest timber buildings next to the central T-junction, those probably of Claudian date, had been cleared away and replaced by a series of structures and alleys, perhaps as part of the same programme of rebuilding in which the street grid was extended (Fig. 6) (Philp 1977, 9–16). This rebuilding can hardly have happened much after *c*. AD 55 since one of the walls put up at this time had been painted four times before its destruction in AD 60.

Although the main part of the early city was on Cornhill, occupation had also extended to cover the western slopes of the Walbrook valley at an early date; certain classes of pre-Flavian pottery are found with sufficient frequency to suggest that this area was occupied before *c*. AD 69. Roads found in excavations at Milk Street, King Street, Gutter Lane and 24–25 Ironmonger Lane were perhaps in place by the time of the fire of AD 60, although it is not yet clear if the traces of fire destruction found on these sites were due to the Boudiccan revolt or an unrecorded fire of the early Flavian period (Norton 1982; Rowsome 1987; Perring and Roskams forthcoming; Frere 1989, 305). The road at Ironmonger Lane sealed a Neronian pit and could have been contemporary with the other streets of *c*. AD 55; Neronian finds were also found in the early roadside ditches at Milk Street.

By the time of the Boudiccan fire the town centre had piped water. An iron collar used to bind a wooden water-main was found in a roadside pipe trench sealed by debris likely to date to AD 60 (Philp 1977, 15). Later water-pipes have been found on several sites close to Cornhill (Wacher 1978; and more recently beneath second-century streets around the forum) and it seems likely that natural springs somewhere immediately to the north were exploited (Wilmott 1982b). This early attention to water supply, like the planned road system, shows London to have been a carefully governed community.

Most of the buildings of pre-Flavian London had wattle and daub walls, earth floors and thatch roofs, whilst window glass was rarely, if ever, used. Some fragments of red- and green-painted wall plaster were recovered from beneath the Boudiccan destruction debris in the town centre and Purbeck marble had also been used in a pre-Flavian building (Pritchard 1988, 185). One of the buildings in the area to the west of the Walbrook, at Queen Victoria Street, had brickearth walls and a tile and concrete floor (*opus signinum*) (Richardson 1988, 387). A cesspit on one side of

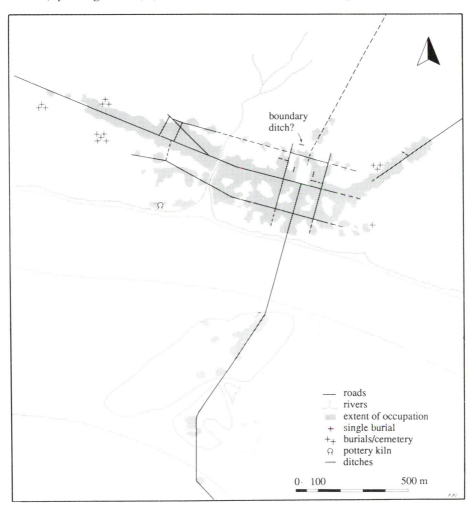

FIG. 5 Pre-Flavian London, showing the extent of development in *c.* AD 60. A planned town, with streets laid out on both sides of the Walbrook, had been established before the destruction of the city during the Boudiccan revolt.

the building contained an impressive collection of broken pre-Flavian tableware, and this was obviously a house of note. Cement floors and painted walls are rarely found in pre-Flavian buildings in Britain, so London may have boasted some of the finest Romano-British houses of the period.

Part of a new building in the centre of town had walls of dried clay bricks over stone foundations, and buildings in the legionary fortress at Colchester were built in a remarkably similar fashion. One of the rooms had housed a stock of grain, probably imported from the Mediterranean or the Near East, at the time of its destruction in AD 60 (Fig. 6) (Boddington and Marsden 1987; Straker 1987). In other times Roman Britain produced grain for export, and the imported grain must surely reflect the specific problems of ensuring supply in a recently conquered province. We cannot know if this grain was waiting to be sent forward to feed the army or was being stored against the needs of the newly established urban communities. It must surely, however, have been imported on public rather than private initiative; the extraordinary distance travelled by this crop only makes sense if it were state property and had moved along state-organized supply lines. The building in which the grain was stored was built to unusually high standards, using techniques elsewhere employed in military buildings, on a site later occupied by a public building (the second forum was eventually built here). This was possibly a public building.

Three phases of Neronian timber buildings and an important collection of rubbish from a nearby pottery kiln were found close to the Thames waterfront on the west side of the Walbrook, at Sugar Loaf Court. There

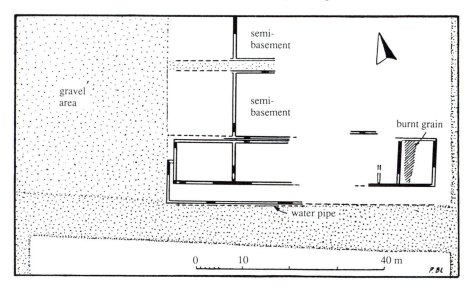

FIG. 6   A plan of buildings adjacent to the gravelled area at the town centre at the time of the Boudiccan revolt (based on drawings by Marsden and Boddington).

FIG. 7 An onyx intaglio, one of four found in a rubbish pit excavated at Eastcheap. It shows a pair of clasped hands and was intended for a betrothal ring. The name ALBA had been scratched on to the surface of the gem in the first stage of marking it out for a dedication, but the stone appears to have been discarded unfinished.

were parts of waste vessels, and amorphous lumps of burnt clay likely to have come from kiln linings, in the rubbish. The pottery, which must have been made close by, was of a type which has been found on a few of the earliest sites in London but is rarely seen in Flavian and later contexts. The styles of pottery produced suggest the hand of an immigrant potter who had perhaps previously worked in the area of western Switzerland or near Lyon (Tyers in Davies and Richardson forthcoming). It is unusual to find kilns inside towns and it is possible that production had started here at a time when the area was still outside the settlement.

Evidence of industrial activity has been found on several other sites in the early city. At 5–12 Fenchurch Street, in the very heart of the town, pits associated with pre-Flavian timber buildings contained a modest amount of industrial waste; some small-scale iron and bronze working seems to have taken place near by (Hammer 1985, 9). A pit at Gateway House, on the western side of town, contained waste material from glass-blowing (Shepherd 1986, 141–3). Four intaglios found in another pre-Flavian pit, this one at 23–29 Eastcheap, may have been from the workshop of a merchant in gems (Fig. 7). There were some stylistic links between the stones and on one the owner's name had been sketched out but not executed (Henig 1984a, 11–15). It is clear that a variety of craftsmen, at least some of whom were immigrant, had soon settled in London.

London, like other Romano-British towns of this period, seems to have been a functional place with few frills. There is little to suggest that the local élite had yet been drawn into city life and the urban population was likely to have been dominated by merchants and craftsmen, many of whom may have considered themselves as only temporarily resident. With no competition for public office, with no sense of civic identity or permanence, the buildings and symbols of Classical Rome had little social value. There was as yet no call for the monumental public buildings which we normally expect to find in a Roman town. The more tangible symbols of success, the jewels and finery for which we do have some evidence, were perhaps proving more popular.

The cemeteries and suburbs of the early town

By AD 60 London was a large and successful place, and had grown far beyond the small area on Cornhill where it may have begun (Fig. 5). This growth seems to have been regulated, if not planned, and new boundaries may have been established. We do not know for certain where the dead of this period were buried but it seems likely that the cemeteries of the later first century were already in use. Four such cemeteries have been fairly reliably located within the line of the later town wall. Three were on Ludgate Hill: at St Paul's Cathedral, Warwick Square and St Martin-le-Grand; and the fourth was in the area of Billiter Street close to the Colchester Road (Shepherd forthcoming; Marsden 1980, 24). All are likely to have been small nucleated cemeteries behind house-plots along the main roads out of town, a pattern typical of roadside settlements (Smith 1987, 115–18). Only the cemetery at Warwick Square has been studied in any detail and this contained some very high-quality burials indeed. These included a variety of ceramic, glass and lead cinerary urns, one of which showed a charioteer in relief, a carved porphyry urn, which also contained a Claudian coin, and a double burial in an amphora (Marsden 1980, 76–7).

Cemeteries are not the only source of information for early city boundaries. Much can also be made of irregularities in street alignments since roads were frequently deflected from their line where they crossed into town. A kink in the line of the Roman west road (Newgate Street), just to the east of the area of known cemeteries, has long been considered evidence for an early city boundary (see Bentley 1985 for the most recent restatement of this argument). Unfortunately the case for the existence of this kink is not entirely convincing; it is possible to draw a straight line from Newgate to the Walbrook and find that the only suggested deviations from this line are due to gravel surfaces which could have been in adjacent forecourts. The western boundary of a mid first-century London must have lain to the east of the St Martin-le-Grand cemetery and, given the extent and character of pre-Flavian occupation, is likely to have been to the west of the lines of Milk Street and Bread Street. The northern boundary of the early city is most likely to have been somewhere close to the road found at 24–25 Ironmonger Lane, for the streets to the north of this line were not laid out until the second century. It is perhaps significant that the later Roman amphitheatre would have been just outside the north-west angle of a city with such boundaries; amphitheatres were commonly sited just outside Roman towns (*see* Fig. 31). It is just possible that a ditch found in excavations at 66–73 Cornhill had been dug to mark the north boundary of the first-century city (Fig. 5). This U-shaped feature was some 3m wide and had been filled *c*. AD 85 (Evans and James 1983, 21). The eastern side of town was probably somewhere between Mincing Lane and Mark Lane. Traces of roadside buildings have shown that the Colchester road continued into town on the Aldgate High Street alignment to the junction of Fenchurch Street and Mark Lane (Guy n.d.), and late first-century burials have also been found this far into town. The buildings and streets to the west of Mincing Lane were, however, on the same orientation as the centrally planned area.

Extensive areas of ribbon development were soon established along the principal roads out of town. By AD 60 buildings had reached a point nearly 1 km west of the town centre on the road to Silchester and Verulamium, extended 600 m to the east of the centre on the road to Colchester and were found approximately 1.4 km to the south along the Kent road (Perring and Roskams forthcoming; Chapman and Johnson 1973; Dean 1980). To the north of the river the streets were fairly crowded with houses and many of these are likely to have been shops and workshops; small quantities of industrial waste have been found on many sites. At Newgate Street the pre-Flavian roadside buildings, which included some circular huts, were built in British rather than Roman fashion. At Arcadia Buildings a bowl furnace and fragments of crucible, of a type considered more native than Roman, were found with the earliest buildings; bronze and brass alloys had been worked (Dean 1980). The more peripheral parts of the town seem to have attracted indigenous settlers who were presumably making a living from servicing the needs of the busy traffic along the principal streets. Elsewhere in Southwark pre-Flavian levels contain a lot of pottery but there is comparatively little evidence for accompanying structures; much of the Kent road may instead have been flanked by temporary markets (Sheldon 1981, 67). The flavour of the area is suggested by finds from the pre-Flavian roadside ditch excavated at

201–211 Borough High Street. This feature contained a number of lamb skulls, which suggest that animals had been brought to the site and slaughtered near by, mixed with the remains of plants normally found on fairly open ground (Ferretti and Graham 1978, 63). At 15–23 Southwark Street a pre-Flavian muddy patch had conserved the stamp of a number of cattle hoof-prints (Beard and Cowan 1988).

The evidence of the roadside development testifies to the importance of Watling Street to early London but also shows that the road to Colchester saw significant use. By contrast Ermine Street, the road north to Lincoln, seems to have been little used at this time; several sites have been excavated in this area but few have produced evidence of pre-Flavian occupation. Part of a timber building destroyed in the Boudiccan fire has been found next to the earliest gravel surfaces of Ermine Street at 28–32 Bishopsgate (Evans and James 1983). This building, less than 300 m from the town centre, represents the northernmost extreme of development along the street. Pre-Flavian banked enclosures found on the same site may have surrounded gardens of some kind.

The London destroyed in AD 60 seems, therefore, to have been a place with a regularly planned centre and very considerable ribbon development along its main arterial roads. It was a large and populous place; estimates based on the numbers slain during the Boudiccan revolt suggest that the city may have had as many as 30,000 inhabitants (Frere 1987a, 253). This can only serve as a very rough guide, and a lower figure seems more likely; but there can be no doubt that, if judged by its size, the city was a great success.

Military and civilian in the foundation of London

The army is widely seen as having been the main catalyst in the creation of Roman towns in Britain. In the case of London discussion departs from the premise, reasonable but unproven, that the armies of Claudius crossed the Thames in the vicinity of London and that a fort must have been placed hereabouts to control the crossing. Prior to the investigation of the streets leading to the Southwark bridgehead it was held likely that there had been a conquest-phase fort beneath the later Roman city, probably on Cornhill (Merrifield 1965, 34–5; Chapman and Johnson 1973, 71). The merchants and other civilians found in the London of AD 60 might therefore have been attracted to the site by the prospect of military spending and protection. Important communities grew up around forts on the Rhine for precisely these reasons. When the armies were moved to more forward positions in *c.* AD 50 many forts of the south-east were made redundant and abandoned. Civilian communities which had grown up around the gates of some forts were now well established and could be promoted into self-governing communities in order to fill the administrative gap left by the departing army.

It now seems probable, however, that London was not established until later in the Claudian period and that the settlement on the Cornhill, although about the right size for a fort, is unlikely to have been defended. For both of these reasons it is difficult to sustain the argument that this was the site of a fort. The ditches near Aldgate do not offer a credible alternative; this was at most a very small establishment placed subordinate to the Cornhill settlement. It has also been suggested that another small camp could have been built to the west of London, by the Fleet valley, although the evidence for this is not convincing (Merrifield 1983, 36–7; Grimes 1968).

We cannot avoid the fact that some kind of Claudian fort is likely to have been established in the London area, if not beneath the City then elsewhere. Although the topography of the area and the logic of the historical context suggest that some sites are more likely than others, we have no direct archaeological evidence for this putative fort (Morris 1982, 78; Fuentes 1985). The important question, however, is not whether or not there was an earlier fort but whether London was a child of that fort. If London was born around AD 50–55, and this is what the evidence leads us to believe, it was born too late; the army had probably already moved on.

An alternative hypothesis has it that the origins of London were entirely civilian; that 'London began not at the nod of a ruler, but through the shrewdness of merchants' (Haverfield 1911). This argument, long unfashionable, has recently been revived (as Marsden 1980, 17–26). It is difficult to believe that London, military or civilian, had been founded without the direct involvement of the provincial administration. In the first place London could only have been reached by fairly considerable feats of civil engineering (Hammerson and Sheldon 1987, 167–8). Projects of this sort were not the consequence of private initiative unless there were already a rich and established community to hand, hardly the case of London. We also know, from the events of AD 60, that the army and state were represented in London from an early date (see further below). The site has also produced many small pieces of military equipment, and although most of these were lost during later periods in the town's history a few have been found in early levels on Cornhill and in Southwark (Hammer 1985, 13; Upson and Pye 1987, 117; Hammerson and Sheldon 1987).

Southwark, where so much of the vital evidence has been found, is similar in several respects to the pre-Flavian industrial and commercial site at Sheepen, outside the legionary fort and succeeding Roman colony at Colchester (Niblett 1985, 24–5). This roadside settlement was the site of much metalworking; and scattered through the site were numerous pieces of military equipment together with dozens of the imitation bronze coins issued to the troops. The finds from the site were both plentiful and of high quality when compared to those from contemporary levels in the town itself. This was a busy suburb largely dedicated to the needs of the army; so too was Southwark.

The area on Cornhill was a more organized settlement and finds closest parallel in the military supply depots of the period, such as those at Richborough and Fishbourne. Richborough had started life as a defended Claudian camp, but during the 50s its ditches were filled in and a regular grid of metalled roads laid out over the site. Timber buildings, many of them probably warehouses, were built up to these streets (Cunliffe 1968, 234–43). Earliest London stands close comparison with the undefended supply base at Richborough and was in a position where a base would have been badly needed (Fig. 2). After *c.* AD 50 the south-east was considered won and military attention turned to the Welsh borders; for the decade to AD 60 most military traffic in Britain headed west and north-west. It would have passed through London, along the Thames or along Watling Street, and goods are likely to have been transferred from river to road at this point. London was built at exactly the time when this need would have become most pressing, and the roadside suburbs and markets, which by AD 60 stretched for nearly 2.5 km along Watling Street, witness the importance of this traffic. Heavy traffic along Watling Street may also be reflected in the distribution pattern of early pottery made in kilns at Brockley Hill, between London and Verulamium (*see* Fig. 18); these wares are commonly found on sites in north Kent and the Midlands, areas linked by Watling Street, but are much rarer on the south and east coasts.

London is first described, in connection with the events of AD 60, as a place best known for its commerce (Tacitus, *Annals* xiv , 32). The words that Tacitus used, *copia negotiatorum et commeatum*, suggest the presence of prosperous merchants and financiers and the busy movement of goods and supplies. If this were the case, if London were truly a thriving commercial centre at the heart of the province's trade and supply routes, it ought to have had a busy port. Excavations on the waterfront, just downstream of the likely site of the bridge, have failed to find any recognizable trace of an early port. At Pudding Lane a modest gravel embankment, a few timber piles, and spreads of flint and chalk were found over the foreshore, but the first serious attempt at foreshore revetment has been dated by dendrochronology to *c.* AD 70 (Milne 1985). It should be noted, however, that most Roman ports were very simple affairs with few, if any, man-made facilities (Houston 1988). Where possible boats would have been drawn up on to the foreshore and unloaded from there, and where this was not practicable boats would have been anchored near by and off-loaded into lighters. It is true that later in

London's Roman history extensive quays were built but these should not be seen as a necessary prerequisite for the growth of the port; the fact that the Flavian port was better organized and more impressively presented does not necessarily have any implications for the volume of trade handled.

It is perhaps more significant that early types of pottery seem comparatively rare on the foreshore around the bridgehead, since the main area of early settlement was set higher up the river bank. The evidence for early buildings and pottery manufacture at Sugar Loaf Court might suggest that the early waterfront activity was more intense further upstream; the most important area for beaching ships might have been around the Walbrook mouth, an important part of the port in later times.

In the absence of archaeological evidence for port installations we must turn instead to the evidence of traded goods. The store of grain described earlier in this chapter was a fortunate find, but most of the goods which passed through London will have left no trace; the principal British export of the period was quite possibly the slave, a merchandise for which we have virtually no archaeological evidence. Imported pottery can, however, be used as a crude measure of the directions and scale of trade. London stands little comparison with the main ports of the Mediterranean. Britain remained firmly peripheral to Roman trade routes, despite the influence of military supply: but London seems to have imported far more Roman pottery than any other British town: 20–25 per cent of pottery found in the first-century city was imported, whereas for most Romano-British towns the figure is *c.* 10 per cent or less (Fulford 1987). It has also been noted that the Samian from the Boudiccan fire debris at London looks 'newer' than that from contemporary levels in Verulamium and Colchester (Millett 1987, 106). This could reflect the fact that London was a newer site, where fewer old pieces were in circulation, but might also indicate that London was better supplied with the latest Samian products and that its port played a more important part in the Samian trade. On sites in the centre of London the Samian imports are estimated to make up some 20–25 per cent of all vessels discarded in pre-Boudiccan levels; even in the poorer suburbs slightly over 10 per cent of the pots of this date were Samian (Rhodes 1986, 202–3). By contrast, Samian only accounted for 1.42 per cent of estimated vessels from deposits earlier than AD 60 in the small town at Chelmsford in Essex. If the Samian coming into London arrived virtually free of carriage charge it would have been cheap and easily available, hence its frequency on even the lowest status sites of the city. Elsewhere distribution and marketing costs had to be added to the London price, and Samian was consequently more precious and more scarce.

It is clear from the archaeological evidence that the London of AD 60 was a town, not simply some army depot. The change from depot to town may have been easily achieved. It must be remembered that military supply was largely in the hands of private contractors, and the presence of a supply base would have encouraged the growth of busy mercantile suburbs. Growth was not only suburban and haphazard; the layout of a carefully planned street system *c*. AD 55 suggests that a conscious decision had been made to convert the site into a town. The Roman administration perhaps preferred to organize army supply through the merchant community of a civilian settlement; it was certainly government policy of the period to establish towns where this was practicable.

Roman towns could be administered in a variety of ways; the most important distinction was between those towns which were self-governing and those which were not. The main kinds of chartered towns were *coloniae* and *municipia*, of which the former were considered more prestigious. The lesser self-governing communities were the *civitates*, or tribes, who retained 'native' administrative structures and whose administrative centres are generally referred to as '*civitas* capitals'. London seems not to have had independent status at the time of the revolt of AD 60. Tacitus in his brief description of the pre-revolt settlement states that London, unlike Colchester, was not a *colonia*. Since he also describes Verulamium as a *municipium*, but makes no such claim for London, it is doubted that London was a *municipium* either. The writings of Suetonius reinforce such doubts by mentioning that only two cities were destroyed by Boudiccan rebels — it is assumed that he was referring to the chartered towns. London was not in a position to have been a *civitas* capital and if not ruled from elsewhere remained under the direct control of the military government; it would have been considered a *vicus*. Settlements of merchants and traders outside Roman forts, although nominally under military control, were often given a considerable degree of autonomy, with developed administrative structures. It has been suggested that there may have been a sufficiently large body of Roman citizens resident at London for these to have been brought together to form an authority responsible for the internal affairs of the community (Haverfield 1911).

London was closely linked with provincial administration from the start. The *procurator*, responsible for imperial property and most fiscal matters, was almost certainly based in London by AD 60. It is quite possible that he had been a moving force behind the foundation of London and he would certainly have worked closely with the leading businessmen and their representatives, people who would have held contracts to manage some of the taxes, mines and estates under his jurisdiction. It has also been suggested, on the grounds of probability rather than from any hard evidence, that the provincial governor had a base in London from its inception (Salway 1985, 70–1).

The site of London had one further advantage to Rome: no local community. The site, although central to the province and its communication systems, was on the border between several neighbouring tribal areas. There was no local landowning élite likely to have felt offended or threatened by the comparatively independent merchant classes, and the interests of province and empire could be served free of pressure to favour the needs of a local community. The site of London would have given merchants and administrators greater freedom than they would have been likely to find elsewhere. Rome seems to have been aware of the advantages of neutral sites, and made something of a habit of establishing principal administrative cities at coastal or estuarine sites on the boundaries between polities (Drinkwater 1975, 139–40; Salway 1985, 70). Some of these sites were also first developed as centres for trade and supply, as conduits for long-distance trade. Before the foundation of London this had happened at Lyon, and later it was to happen at York. Given these parallels it is possible that London had been chosen as a potential centre for imperial administration from the start.

2 The creation of the Flavian city (*c.* AD 60−100)

The Boudiccan revolt and its aftermath

London had grown with spectacular speed to become the largest town of Roman Britain but its initial success was brought sharply to a halt by the revolt of AD 60. Revolts were not uncommon in newly conquered Roman provinces and the early stages of Romanization were especially delicate; local aristocracies had yet to be drawn into Roman administrative systems whilst the new cities and merchant classes had done much to undermine the traditional basis of social power.

When the revolt started the governor was on campaign in north Wales. The colonists at Colchester, the first city to be threatened, called on the *procurator* Decianus Catus for help. Only 200 troops were sent to their aid, presumably from forces attached to the *procurator* and stationed with him at London, but these could do little to save the town. Before the revolt was suppressed London, Colchester and Verulamium, the three leading cities of the province, had been burnt to the ground.

Excavations in the City suggest that few buildings, if any, had escaped the fire. It is not yet clear if Southwark was also destroyed, although pre-Flavian burnt debris has been mentioned in some interim reports (Rankov 1982; Bird and Graham 1978, 521: site 29; Marsden 1971, 21). Recovery after the fire was slow, indeed very slow. A spate of recent excavations have shown that most sites were left vacant for about a decade after the revolt (Milne 1985, 143; Perring and Roskams forthcoming; Rowsome 1987, 22; Williams in preparation). Some streets were abandoned for this decade and on at least one site, 25−26 Lime Street, redevelopment was delayed until the late Trajanic period. In most areas it is likely that the ruins had been tidied up a bit, at least no bodies were left lying around, but that was that.

One of the few finds which can reliably be dated to this period is the tombstone of Julius Alpinus Classicianus, *procurator* of the province of Britain, who died in office and was buried in London. Classicianus succeeded Decianus Catus and played an important part in post-revolt restoration. His tombstone was found re-used in the base of a late Roman bastion at Trinity Square (Cottrill 1936). The stone was set up by his wife, Julia Pacata, who was the daughter of Indus, a leading Gaul who had sided with Rome during a revolt of AD 21. From the evidence of his name it seems likely that Classicianus was also a Gaul. The London that Classicianus saw was most probably a sparsely occupied settlement with a few timber buildings surrounded by large open wastes. Until recently it was thought that a stone building, perhaps a public building, had been built on a central site in the years immediately after the fire, but a recent re-evaluation of the evidence has shown that this is unlikely to have been the case (Marsden 1987, 22). Most of the people who had been living in London before AD 60 did not return. It is possible that the potter working near Sugar Loaf Court was among the missing; hence the rarity of his wares in later contexts.

Interim reports suggest that a group of large earth-filled trenches found in excavations at 15–23 Southwark Street were dug in the 60s (Beard and Cowan 1988, 376). The trenches are unusual but may have been foundation or robbing trenches, possibly for a stone building that was never finished. Could this have been a construction programme halted by the revolt? This site may have housed a public building from the 70s, and it is possible that these trenches too were associated with a public building.

These were also poor years at Verulamium (Frere 1983b, 8; 1987a, 76–7) and the factors which had promoted urban growth in the years to AD 60 were no longer in operation. The problem seems partly to have been one of confidence. Suetonius mentions that Nero had considered evacuating Britain, although we are not told when, and if the future of the province was uncertain then the future of its towns would have been equally bleak. The period was also one of comparative military inactivity; according to Tacitus the legions became despoiled and impoverished, in which case the supply routes through London might have been little used.

The first forum

The Flavian period saw renewed activity throughout Britain, and in London was marked by a vigorous building programme. The principal public building of the Romano-British town, the most evident demonstration of urban status, was the forum. The forum site in London has recently been the subject of a valuable study by Peter Marsden which provides the basis for most of the comments which follow (Marsden 1987).

A Flavian forum was built at the heart of the city on Cornhill (Fig. 8). This rectangular complex, 104.5 by 52.7 m, consisted of an open area enclosed on all sides by ranges of rooms. The dominant building was the basilica which occupied the north range of the complex. This was a large

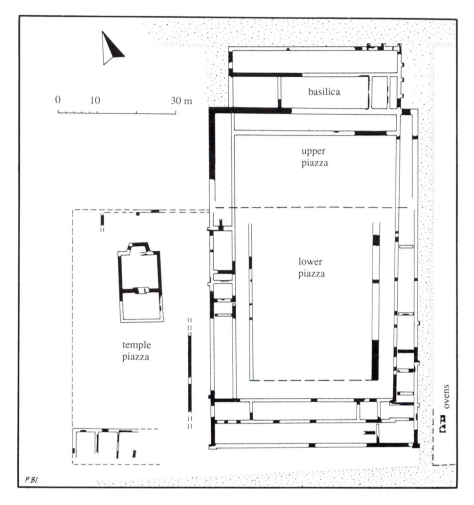

FIG. 8   A suggested plan of the Flavian forum and temple (derived in part from drawings by Marsden).

aisled hall which measured 44 by 22.7 m with a tall central nave, 8.38 m wide, and aisles to the north and perhaps south. It was probably where the council and its officers met, where records were kept, legal disputes settled and civic valuables banked. Cross-walls at the east end of the basilica may have supported a tribunal, a raised dais for the magistrates; at the western end of the building was semi-basement.

The other sides of the forum were surrounded by narrow ranges of rooms which might have been offices, storerooms or shops. On the south these were set behind a portico or range of rooms which had faced on to the street. The exterior walls of the complex were decorated with engaged brick columns or buttresses, and the open space within the forum had almost certainly been divided into two or more courtyards. The northern part of the forum was significantly higher than the rest and a drop of about 1 m must be accommodated somewhere between 79 and 87 Gracechurch Street, an area where there have not yet been any controlled excavations. The perimeter wall of the forum also changes somewhere in the same area; to the north the wall was 1.37 m wide but to the south only 0.86−0.91 m wide. These changes suggest that the complex had been divided into two parts by a terrace wall, or more probably a range of rooms. There would therefore have been a smaller higher-level northern piazza and a larger, lower courtyard to the south. These courtyards might have been used as market-places, but their main function is likely to have been ceremonial and social; they were public meeting places. Substantial foundations within the lower piazza may have supported the colonnade of an inner portico; a slight difference in construction technique suggests that this might have been built in a later phase. A series of brick piers found in the southern part of the forum was more certainly of a later construction phase, in which most of the ranges around the lower piazza had been levelled and replaced.

To the west of the forum was a building, most probably a small temple, built in the same fashion as the forum. It was a south-facing structure, with a central room (or *cella*) 8.5 m square, and an angular apse on its north side. The building façade had probably been formed by a portico with two columns, reached by a small flight of steps. A gravelled area around the building was surrounded by the walls of a temple precinct (Marsden 1987; walls 32−35 at 17−19 Gracechurch Street; wall E at All Hallows, Lombard Street; and the earliest stone foundations at 54−58 Lombard Street). These were built in the same style as those of the portico inside the forum, and might similarly have been put up in a later phase. Rooms on the southern side of the precinct had perhaps faced on to the street to the south.

The forum was a Flavian construction, but there is some uncertainty about when in this period it was built. One of its walls had cut through a rubbish pit which contained a coin of AD 71, and rubbish beneath a street on the east side of the building contained Samian of *c.* 75−85 (Marsden, 1987, 73). Marsden has argued that this rubbish predated the forum which he suggests was built in the early 80s. The street was, however, a minor affair and could have been added when the forum was already in use, as was proposed by its excavator (Philp 1977). At least one other public building was probably built in London in the period AD 72−74 (see further below) and it would be surprising if the forum were not one of the earlier public building projects to have been tackled. The archaeological evidence is imprecise but the forum need not be as late as Marsden proposes. A date in the mid 70s would make this the first in a series of British forums; an inscription from the building at Verulamium clearly dates its dedication to AD 79 (Frere 1983b), and the timber basilica at

Silchester is suggested to date to the 80s (Fulford 1985, 39−81). The first London forum, with its elongated double courtyard and temple precinct, resembles Romano-Gallic forums; this too might hint at an early date.

The construction of the forum implies that London now had a sense of civic identity; it is possible that the town had been made a *municipium* or even *colonia* at this point. It is worth noting, however, that forums could be built in towns which were not autonomous. Alesia, which lay in territory administered from Autun, provides an example; the forum here would have been used in the affairs of the *vicus* but authority rested with the magistrates who met in Autun. Archaeological opinion remains divided about the exact status of London at this time (Frere 1987a, 76; Wilkes 1981, 415).

The waterfront

One of the most impressive achievements of the Flavian period was the construction of the port of Roman London. This area has also been the subject of a valuable recent study, in this case by Gustav Milne, and it is from his work that the following summary derives (Milne 1985). The slopes to the Thames were terraced, in a major engineering operation, to allow occupation to extend over previously awkward terrain. The lower terrace, which was up to 24 m wide and raised some 2 m above flood level, was revetted by timber quays laid out across the pre-Flavian fore-shore. Massive squared oak timbers, up to 8.5 m long and as much as 480 by 730 mm in cross-section, were used in this construction. Jetties and

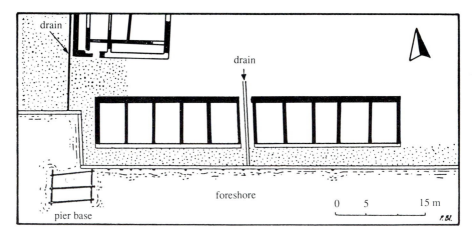

FIG. 9   Plan of buildings and quays along the Thames (based on drawings by Bateman and Milne). The building to the north, found in excavations at 37−40 Fish Street Hill, may have been earlier than the other features illustrated. The timber pier base built over the foreshore might have supported a bridge over the Thames.

FIG. 10 The late first-century waterfront at Pudding Lane showing part of the timber quay and open-fronted storage buildings illustrated in Fig. 9.

open-framework landing stages were also built. Altogether a maximum length of *c.* 620 m can be suggested for the first-century waterfront. Timbers from excavations at several points demonstrate that the entire waterfront had been built *c.* AD 70–90, with some parts certainly in place by AD 79. Most of the quays were up-river of the bridge, some to the west of the Walbrook.

Recent work in the area of the Walbrook mouth, perhaps as much as 200 m across where it flowed into the Thames, shows it to have been a complex area of quays and jetties. Excavations on the east side of the Walbrook, beneath Cannon Street station, have uncovered parts of north–south aligned revetments some 50 m upstream (M. Burch and J. Hill, personal communication; see also DUA 1987, 207 for equivalent revetments on the west side of the Walbrook). This area may have seen some of the earliest and latest Roman waterfront activity and was perhaps one of the more important parts of the port.

Fragments from several small vessels suitable for the river and traffic along the east coast have been found in and around London. These included lighters, barges and sailing ships. Boats would still have beached on the river foreshore but the quays provided working platforms, above tide level, where goods could be stacked during loading and unloading operations.

Warehouses and other buildings were built on and near the waterfront (Fig. 9). One of the earliest of these was a large stone building (at least 16 by 16 m) built *c.* AD 60–75, a corner of which was found in excavations at 37–40 Fish Street Hill (Bateman 1986, 233–8). This was built next to the bridge approach road but some distance behind the waterfront. The earliest buildings by the river had not survived but a series of slightly later buildings were well preserved. At Pudding Lane the original Flavian landing stage had been replaced by a timber quay *c.* AD 90–95 and the terrace behind this was occupied by two stone buildings, perhaps transit sheds (Fig. 10). The buildings measured *c.* 25 by 6 m and had been divided into five bays, *c.* 4.3 m wide, each floored in timber. The buildings, which had been tile roofed, were open fronted and had perhaps originally been closed by removable wooden shutters.

The scale of London's port was very modest indeed when compared to some of the massive harbour works associated with the Mediterranean grain trade, but these were the exceptional product of large-scale state intervention and subsidy. For a frontier supply town, as London was likely to have been, it was endowed with an unusually large and handsome port. There is at present no reason to believe that this was bettered elsewhere in Britain.

The south bank of the Roman river was largely destroyed by medieval riverine erosion. At the Winchester Palace site, however, an early revetment of close-set piles survived, and shows that the waterfront here had advanced north in the period AD 80–120 (Yule 1989, 32). No massive timber quays similar to those on the north bank have yet been found in Southwark, although recent work at Guy's Hospital has revealed part of a slightly more modest timber wharf (*The Times*, 6 Dec. 1989). Excavations on the

FIG. 11   The remains of a timber warehouse, built *c.* AD 100, and found in a remarkable state of preservation during recent excavations at the Courage Brewery site in Southwark.

Courage Brewery site have also uncovered a remarkably well-preserved timber warehouse built *c.* AD 100 (Dillon 1988, 1989) (Fig. 11). This half-cellared structure, at least 11 m long by 4.75 m wide, had a solid oak-plank floor and oak walls which stood at least 1.6 m high; the roof was made of wooden shingles which had been nailed into place. It was entered by a wooden ramp. It is now clear that harbour activities were not confined to the impressive waterfront terrace on the north bank.

The scale and character of the waterfront on the north bank imply that it was the result of public, not private, initiative. It was developed in the years after *c.* AD 70, and had therefore been added to a town which may previously have been an important port. It was an 'optional extra' which improved the aspect and organization of both harbour and town.

Baths and palaces on the Thames

Not all of the buildings set over the new waterside terraces were stores and warehouses; some of the city's more prestigious and imposing public buildings were also built by the Thames. One of the better known is the bathing establishment at Huggin Hill. This site was set near natural springs on one of the terraces above the Thames, close to the likely western limit of the city (*see* Fig. 25). Recent work at Dominant House, on the west side of the complex, has added significantly to our knowledge of the form and evolution of the building (Marsden 1976; Rowsome and Woolridge 1989; Rowsome 1990). Since work is still in progress it has not been possible to prepare a plan to accompany this part of the text. The principal part of the early baths consisted of a single range of rooms set parallel to the river. Bathers would have entered the complex via the unheated rooms which were located at the east end of the building. A heated room, probably a warm room, was set in the middle of the range and a hot room was found at its west end; this measured approximately 13 by 6m with apses to south and west (Fig. 12). The latest investigations on this site seem to offer broad confirmation of the date of *c.* AD 80 suggested for the baths by Marsden, although work on the analysis of the finds continues.

Another public building complex was set over terraces above the river on the eastern side of the Walbrook, in the angle between revetments of the Walbrook and those of the Thames (Fig. 13). This is the site presently occupied by Cannon Street station and the streets to its east. Past investigations in this area have been hampered by enormously difficult working conditions and as a consequence our knowledge is patchy. Marsden, reporting on work here, came to the conclusion that this was the site of a Flavian palace, possibly the palace of the provincial governor (Marsden 1975, 1978). This is indeed one interpretation the evidence will

FIG. 12   General view, looking south, of the hot room uncovered at the west end of the Huggin Hill baths in 1988.

bear, but it is not the only one. The remains considered by Marsden covered an area *c.* 130 m north–south and more than 72 m east–west but it is not certain that these were all part of a single building complex, or all of the same date.

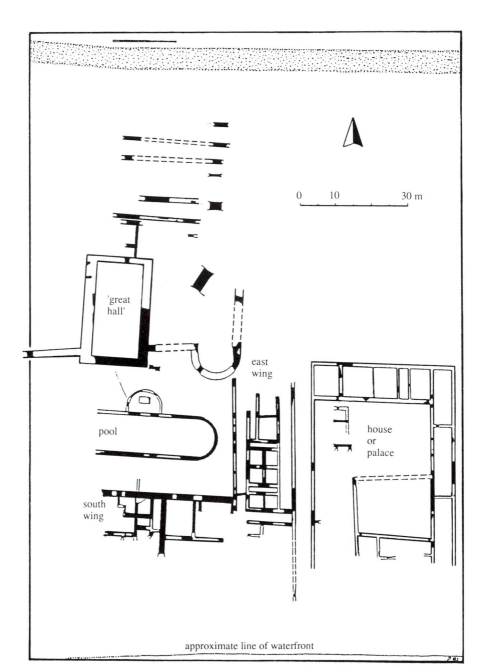

FIG. 13 The public building complex in the area of Cannon Street station, the so-called governor's palace (after Marsden).

At the heart of the area was a courtyard within which was a sunken apsidal-ended structure about 10.6 m wide and over 31.1 m long, with foundations about 1.8 m thick; this was most probably a pool. A smaller apse added on to the north side of the pool contained a rectangular masonry base, perhaps for a statue. No dating evidence was recovered from this area but the monumental scale of the pool suggests that it was associated with a series of massively built rooms to the north. The most impressive of these was a great 'hall' which measured 24.38 by 13.1 m, and had side walls with 3 m wide foundations; the end walls were narrower. The floor was of plain mortar except in the northern part of the 'hall' where part of a hypocaust survived; it is not clear if this was built during a later phase of alteration or indicates that the 'hall' had been divided into two rooms when built. A pit beneath this room contained Flavian pottery. On the east side of the 'hall' was an equally massive room, of contemporary construction, with a projecting apse; to the north were rooms with hypocaust floors. Marsden suggests that these were the main staterooms of the palace.

To the east of the courtyard was a range of rooms, some heated by hypocausts, flanked by corridors; according to Marsden these may have been administrative offices. Pits beneath this range contained no material later than Flavian. South of the courtyard and pool was a building on a lower level, the rear wall of which retained the upper terrace. Some of the rooms in this building contained fragments of mosaic and hypocaust floors, although these had probably been added in a later phase. Marsden sees this as the residential wing of the palace. Most of the pottery beneath the building on the lower terrace can be dated to the first century, with some later than c. AD 80. Immediately west of these buildings, recent work beneath Cannon Street station has found part of the retaining wall, probably with architectural embellishment, which faced the Thames (M. Burch and J. Hill, personal communication). It is possible that this was part of the river façade presented by the building complex. A column base has also been observed between the buildings and the quayside.

The argument that this site was a palace rests on the assumption that the various remains were contemporary and part of a single complex. If there had been a public building here with extensive residential quarters then the argument for its identification as a palace has considerable weight. The problem is that those rooms which looked residential in the southern and eastern ranges need not have been in the public building or could have been added to it at a later date. The other arguments presented by Marsden, concerning the position and aspect of the building, do not distinguish palaces from other high-status public buildings.

Other functions for this building complex should also be considered. Milne has noted that the southern and eastern ranges may have been used in association with the waterfront, although there is no direct evidence for this (Milne 1985, 130). The courtyard and rooms to the north could perhaps have been part of a temple or baths complex rather than a palace. Mark Burch and Julian Hill have suggested (personal communication) that the foundations of the large 'hall' could have been a temple podium; and an inscription found reused in later foundations near by at Nicholas Lane might arguably have come from a temple dedicated to the imperial cult. The inscription, in letters 15 cm high, has usually been taken to be a dedication to the divinity of the Emperor by the province of Britain (RIB 5), although this depends on a disputable and perhaps anachronistic reconstruction of the text; it is only certain that the province is mentioned. It is also difficult to see how the room with the apse to the east of the great 'hall' would have been accommodated in a temple complex.

The organization and location of the Cannon Street buildings show some similarities with the late Trajanic baths at Conimbriga in Portugal. Here the complex included a *palaestra* (exercise yard) to one side of the baths and a *natatio* (ceremonial pool) to the other; at a lower level there was a garden, with a monumental façade which incorporated two apsidal shelters and looked out on to a river gorge (Alarcão and Étienne, 1977). If part of a bathing establishment then the Cannon Street 'hall' would have been one of the monumental rooms in the principal range of the complex, a large changing room or cold room. The heated rooms would have been to the north and east. The presence of baths at Huggin Hill does not preclude the possibility that there had been other public baths elsewhere — most half-way decent Roman towns were provided with more than one set of baths. In sum the evidence is inconclusive, but the identification of this as the site of the governor's palace is only one of several possibilities and not necessarily the most compelling.

To the east of the Cannon Street public building (east of Suffolk Lane) there was another building which has been interpreted as an associated official residence (also illustrated in Fig. 13). It covered an area 55 by 38 m and contained various ranges of rooms, some with tessellated pavements and mosaics. There was no dating evidence from the building, save for a third-century coin over a floor, but the polychrome mosaics here might be more in keeping with a second-century or later date. There had clearly been a fine town house here but there is little direct evidence to support the suggestion that this was an official building of the Flavian period.

A site which has as good a claim to have been an official residence has been excavated in Southwark, at Winchester Palace. By the end of the first century part of this waterfront site facing the Roman city had been occupied by a large apsidal-ended building constructed of stone and tile. As its excavator, Brian Yule, has pointed out, its size and the early use of masonry suggest that it was a public building (Yule 1989, 33). Early second-century rebuilding on this site incorporated some very sumptuously decorated rooms and these allow the building to be described as palatial. Southwark might have offered certain advantages as a site for an official residence; outside the town proper it would have been easier for the officials attached to the provincial administration to remain independent of the city.

Other public buildings and works in the Flavian town

Another public building in Southwark, close to the line of Watling Street, has tentatively been identified at 15–23 Southwark Street (Beard and Cowan 1988, 376–8). A large stone building, with a courtyard at least 18 m across, included at least three rooms with tessellated pavements. Piles used in the foundations were felled in the years 72, 73 and 74, and date the building to AD 74 (Sheldon and Tyers 1983). This building was unusually large and exceptionally well built for the period and this hints at public ownership. This possibility is reinforced by the evidence for a major building project on the site in the AD 60s, and by the discovery here of a number of military objects. The interim report on this building suggests tentatively but plausibly that it could have been a *mansio*, a sort of state guesthouse and coaching inn, although such buildings may also have had other administrative functions.

The early second-century amphitheatre recently identified beneath Guildhall Yard was built over a curved row of posts with associated surfaces which could possibly have been part of an earlier amphitheatre (Heathcote 1989, 48).

Excavations close to the site of the forum, at 5–12 Fenchurch Street, uncovered part of an aisled building with timber and brickearth walls set on gravel and mortar foundations (Hammer 1987, 6–12; Williams in preparation). This unusual building saw frequent repair and alteration, and associated pottery indicates that it was built in the mid 70s and remained standing until the middle of the second century. It probably measured 19 m by at least 11 m, with an aisle 2.2 m wide formed by a row of pier bases on its north side; an aisle to the south is hypothesized (Fig. 14). Partitions had divided the aisles into smaller rooms and others were later added to the sides of the building; one room may have contained a latrine and some contained hearths. A room with an *opus signinum* floor and wall paintings, consisting of an architectural illusionistic scheme with a standing female figure, was added in the early second century (Rhodes 1987b, 169–72). An adjacent room contained amphorae and flagons, but little table ware, and might perhaps have been a kitchen. One possible interpretation of this building is that it had been an enclosed market or *macellum*, with rows of shops set around a central court or nave, but it

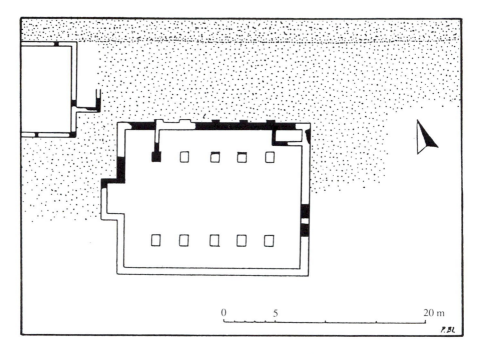

0 5 20 m

P.BL

FIG. 14 A reconstruction of the plan of the aisled building found in Fenchurch Street (after Hammer).

compares poorly with covered markets in other Romano-British towns. Fredrike Hammer, who directed excavations on the site, instead favours its interpretation as a meeting place for a *collegium* or guild.

It is also possible that the Fenchurch Street building was not a public building at all. Aisled buildings are commonly found on villa and other rural sites, and a building of this type was built in the Roman town of Cirencester, although in a later context and close to the edge of town (McWhirr 1986, 71−8). It is unlikely, however, that a type of building normally associated with agricultural activity was built close to the heart of London at a time when the city was crowded with shops and houses.

The Flavian period witnessed a number of improvements and additions to the road system, although the basics of the pre-Flavian system were left intact; most early Flavian growth was absorbed by the empty spaces left after the Boudiccan revolt (Fig. 15). A road first seen at 9 St Clare Street, where it was dated Flavian if not earlier, and more recently recorded at 80−84 Leadenhall Street, was perhaps of this phase; its introduction could explain an early Flavian shift in building alignment at 94−97 Fenchurch Street (Ellis 1985, 117; Heathcote 1989, 50−1; Rivière and Thomas 1987). This road seems to have been set out on the alignment of the Cornhill street grid and could represent a modest northward extension to the gridded area. One of the improvements of this period may have been the construction of a new bridge; part of a braced timber box-structure 7 m across was found in excavations at Pudding Lane and might have been a pier base for a bridge (Milne 1985, 46–53) (*see* Fig. 9). This was probably built *c.* 85–90 and is unlikely to have been the first London bridge. Important alterations were also made in Southwark where it seems likely that several of the water channels through the suburb were blocked off in the Flavian period and the area converted into a peninsula, having previously been an island (Sheldon 1978, 15).

Some roads and lanes were established in the suburbs of this period, as those found in the Paternoster Square development (Shepherd forthcoming), but may have been the consequence of private initiative. Roads out of the city along Bishopsgate and Ludgate Hill had also been laid by the end of the first century, and a narrow lane was laid out in the late first century

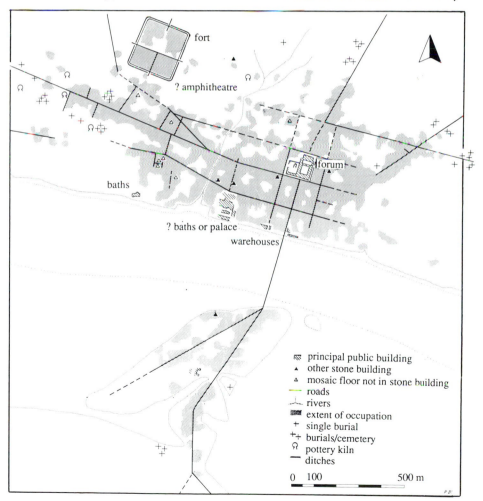

FIG. 15   Flavian London, showing the extent of development in *c.* AD 95.

close to the line later taken by the Roman road through Aldersgate (Williams in preparation; McCann and Orton 1989, 105; DUA 1987, 28, 166; G. Egan, personal communication). The Flavian suburbs seemed much more ordered than their predecessors; the redevelopment of these areas, generally datable to the decade or so after AD 70, may have seen the introduction of organized property boundaries in areas which had previously been poorly regulated street-side sprawls. In some areas the houses of this period, still mostly simple buildings of wood and clay, were now built using different and more Romanized construction techniques (Perring and Roskams forthcoming).

Soldiers and officials

Flavian London retained a distinctly military flavour; finds of military equipment and tombstones witness the presence of a large number of soldiers in the city. The most direct evidence comes not from London but from a fort on Hadrian's Wall. A list, dated *c.* AD 90, found in excavations at Vindolanda, gives the disposition of soldiers seconded from the Cohort of Tungrians stationed there: eleven soldiers and a centurion were at London, sixteen were with the governor and a few were with a certain Ferox, perhaps the *procurator* (Keys 1988, 54).

The governor's administrative staff consisted of 200 or more soldiers detached from the legions. Most of these were *beneficiarii consularis*, men largely concerned with the supervision of supply and logistical support for the army. There were also thirty *speculatores* responsible for the custody and execution of prisoners and delivering dispatches. Further to these the governor had a bodyguard of *equites* and *pedites singulares*, picked men from the cavalry alae and infantry cohorts, probably about 1,000 in all (Hassall 1973, 231–7). Although many of these would have followed the governor on campaign, and in his administrative tours, some were permanently based in London. By the end of the Flavian period the governor must have had his principal base here. A few of these men on special duties are mentioned on tombstones which have been found in London (RIB 19; Painter 1963, 123–8).

The figure of a late first-century legionary soldier or junior officer, originally part of a funerary monument, was found reused in a late Roman bastion added to the town wall at Camomile Street (Fig. 16). The style of the monument was Julio-Claudian but with many Flavian details (Bishop 1983, 31–48; Henig 1978, 120). The effigy, which survived to a height of 1.32 m, showed the deceased wearing a military cloak, fastened by buttons and toggles, over a military tunic and leather apron; he also wore a short sword and scarf. In his left hand he held a scroll and writing tablets; his raised right hand would have held a lance. The tablets and

FIG. 16 The stone effigy of a soldier, perhaps a junior officer employed in administrative duties, from a late first-century funerary monument. Found re-used in a late Roman bastion at Camomile Street.

scroll show him to have been engaged in clerical duties, presumably on the governor's staff.

A stone fort, most probably built to accommodate these soldiers serving on the governor's staff and bodyguard, was first recognized at Cripplegate by Professor Grimes (Grimes 1968, 17—40). There is a circumstantial case to be made for the construction of a fort on this site by *c.* AD 90, at which time it probably lay just outside the north-west corner of the city, behind shops and cemeteries along the main west road (Fig. 15). The fort was rectangular and covered 4.5 ha, which would have made it large enough to house about 1,500–2,000 men. Its defences consisted of a stone wall backed by an earthen rampart and fronted by a V-shaped ditch, the corners of the fort were defended by internal towers and some smaller turrets have also been found along the line of the wall. Part of the west gate was excavated by Grimes and this comprised a double portal flanked by square towers.

The earliest possible date for the fort was provided by a coin of AD 71 found in a pit beneath the rampart bank. Fragments of two stone barracks, with row of rooms about 6.5 m square, flanked by a corridor or veranda, and part of a building with a red tessellated floor and painted wall plaster were recorded inside the fort. These buildings are likely to date to the second century but might possibly have replaced earlier timber structures. Elsewhere in Britain fortresses were being built in stone from *c.* AD 100 (Frere 1987a, 109), although there is no particular reason why London should not have set, rather than followed, the trend. Several features suggest that there had been a fort here by the end of the first century. Large flat-bottomed ditches at 7–12 Aldersgate, about 30m to the west, seem to have aligned on the fort but were filled in the late first to early second century (G. Egan, personal communication; DUA 1987, 28). Similar features, also in disuse by the late first to early second century, may have been found some 30–40 m to the south of the fort at 47–57 Gresham Street (Heathcote 1989, 49). These were perhaps drainage and boundary features laid out around an already extant, and therefore first-century, fort. A fort here might also explain certain peculiarities in the Flavian street pattern, in particular the alignment of the road found at Foster Lane (Blair 1983). A fort might have been here early enough to have accommodated the soldiers we know to have been stationed in London *c.* AD 90.

Remains of a bronze diploma granting citizenship and marriage rights, presumably to a veteran of the Roman auxiliary army, were found at Watling Court in a Flavian town house which had burnt to the ground in the early second century (*see* Fig. 22) (Roxan 1983; Perring and Roskams forthcoming). The document was probably issued *c.* AD 100, perhaps to a soldier who had served on the governor's guard, and there is a distinct possibility that the veteran or his heirs had lived in this house. The clay-walled building contained a series of black and white mosaics, perhaps laid by Italian mosaicists, which are presently the earliest known mosaics from a Romano-British town (Fig. 17) (D. Smith in Perring and Roskams forthcoming). Some of the more evidently prosperous citizens of early Roman London may have been veterans. The city of this period may have contained a modest number of well-decorated town houses; fragments of black and white mosaics likely to date to the late first century have been

FIG. 17 Lifting a late first-century mosaic floor from the town house found at Watling Court.

noted on several other sites, and fragments from a disturbed stone inlay (*opus sectile*) floor were found at 28−32 Bishopsgate (Fig. 15) (Marsden 1976, 43; Boddington 1979, 26; Merrifield 1965, site 106; Frere 1989, 305; Pritchard 1988, 177).

Soldiers and veterans were not the only wealthy residents of Flavian London. A hexagonal tombstone found at Ludgate Hill had been set up to Claudia Martina, a Roman citizen, who had died at the age of 19 (RIB 21). The stone, which from the character of the inscription is likely to date to the late first century, had been dedicated by her widower, Anencletus, a slave of the provincial council. This council was a gathering of representatives from the self-governing communities of the province, largely concerned with the ceremonies of the state cult. The presence of Anencletus, the 'first known British civil servant' (Birley 1979, 145), is another illustration of the importance of the city in the administrative affairs of the province. Society in Roman London may have been dominated by soldiers and freedmen brought to the city by the needs of provincial government.

Who built Flavian London?

The public building programme launched soon after AD 70 had resulted in the complete transformation of the city. The piles used in the building at Southwark Street show that timbers were being felled in preparation for this programme as early as AD 72. Work on the forum started no earlier than this, but could have been under way by the middle of the decade. The earliest parts of the massive waterfront terrace were in place by the end of the 70s, and work on the major public buildings set on the terraces by the river continued for much of the 80s and perhaps to the end of the century. Work seems to have started on administrative buildings and proceeded to the main urban landscaping projects on the north bank, whilst the baths and 'palaces' awaited the new river terraces.

Although individual parts of the scheme may have been privately sponsored it is impossible to believe that this programme of public works was not carefully co-ordinated. It has been suggested that this programme was the consequence of a state decision, supported by imperial patronage, to create a show-piece provincial capital (Salway 1981, 57; Merrifield 1983, 87−8). There is indeed strong evidence that most aspects of provincial administration had been centralized in London by *c.* AD 90, and this might have been planned from the 70s.

The involvement of the state in the rebuilding of London might be indicated by the use of tiles stamped PP.BR.LON, or similar, on public sites of the late first and early second centuries (Marsden 1975, 70−1). The stamp was probably the mark of the 'Procurator of the Province of Britain at London'. There is no convincing evidence, however, that significant use was made of these tiles in the early Flavian building programme, nor is their presence conclusive evidence of state involvement in a project; imperial works (probably in the Brockley Hill area, see Bird 1985) could have produced these bricks for sale to the London building trade. It is often suggested that army staff would have helped out on building programmes of this scale, but the army was very busy elsewhere during much of this period and there is no reason why the project could not have been an entirely civilian matter; architects and engineers could have been brought in from other provinces. The city may have been able to fund some of this building programme from its own resources. If it had inherited extensive public lands from a previous military administration these could soon have been yielding high rents (*see* page 67), and the first city councillors and magistrates may well have been expected to make a generous contribution to city coffers as an entry 'fee'. Ports and markets might also have provided a steady income of tolls and taxes. Elsewhere in the empire limited city income was often compensated for by traditions of individual munificence, and although it is questionable whether such traditions ever really took hold in Britain London may have found rich patrons amongst its soldiers and administrators. In the absence of building dedications we cannot really know who paid for the public buldings of London.

It is notable, however, that the Flavian revival of London seems to have started in the public sector; the public architecture did not reflect the success of London but predicted it. The revival also happened at a significant point in the history of the province. In AD 71, after years of comparative inactivity, the legions were reinforced and a series of major campaigns launched. These campaigns were to continue into the mid 80s and saw the conquest of Wales, the north and much of Scotland. The timing and character of the revival of London might therefore imply that it was the consequence of deliberate policy and was co-ordinated with the programme of military advance. This policy is mentioned by Tacitus, who describes the aid and encouragement given to British communities by the governor Agricola.

As far as London is concerned, the most obvious difference between the planning of *c*. AD 55 and that of *c*. AD 70+ was in the approach to public building. Most of London's new Flavian buildings did not directly serve the needs of the provincial administration, nor indeed of the merchants and traders who seem to have been so important to London's earlier growth. These buildings were instead the necessary symbols and tools of a Roman city which had the institutions and pretensions of self-government. The Flavian policy of advance in Britain was underpinned by a policy of urbanization of which London was one of the earliest and principal beneficiaries.

3 The circumstances of the early Roman city (*c.* AD 70–150)

The hinterland of London

It is probable that most of the tribal territories of south-east Britain were granted some form of local self-government during the 70s and 80s, and the administrative capitals of these areas consequently witnessed a vigorous public building programme. The evidence of the early Flavian forum in London encourages the belief that London too had been given some form of autonomous government, and if this were the case then surrounding lands may also have been attached to the authority of the city. Archaeological opinion has tended to deny London a dependent territory, partly because it was not the capital of a tribal area and partly because its central role in the commercial and administrative life of the province left it in little need of such lands (Rivet 1964, 138). London could have been modelled on Lyon, the administrative capital of Gaul, which was given a very small territory. London, once self-governing, would, however, have had at least some lands; the city could hardly have been left dependent on neighbouring peoples for its burial grounds and public pasture. It has been suggested that these territories might even have been quite extensive (Sheldon and Scharf 1978, 71) and this too is a possibility worth considering.

The early Flavian reorganization of local government in south-east Britain almost certainly saw a fair amount of territorial readjustment (Branigan 1985, 45). In the pre-Roman period areas of tribal influence had fluctuated considerably and it would not have been too difficult to carve a London territory out of surrounding tribal areas. The lands of the Thames estuary, southern Essex and northern Kent were poorly integrated with the areas further to north and south and the Thames had not always served as a boundary (Dunnett 1975, 28; Detsicas 1983, 5; Pollard 1988, 200). These territories would have been easily divorced from Roman administrative units based on Canterbury and Colchester and were in many senses naturally linked to London. To the south of London a large band of Surrey, separated from territories of the Regni by the higher ground of the Weald, was in the economic sphere of London and most awkward to govern from Chichester (Cunliffe 1973, 23).

Temple sites were sometimes found on important boundaries, and temples at Harlow and Farley Heath (near Dorking) could arguably have been at points where several territories met (Fig. 18). A temple precinct and settlement at Springhead on Watling Street could have marked the division between areas based on London and Canterbury, although several alternative sites along Watling Street can also be proposed; for example, at Greenwich where a hilltop building, probably a shrine, was built *c.* AD 100 (Detsicas 1983, 60–76; Sheldon and Yule 1979). A temple site at Titsey, just off the London–Lewes road, could also have been close to the southern boundary of an area attached to London (Rivet 1964, 145;

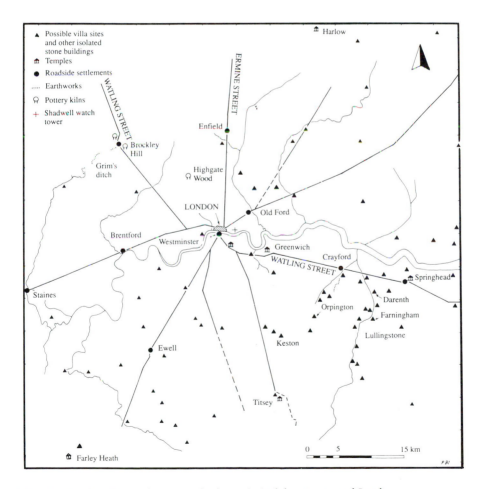

FIG. 18 Roads, villas, settlements and other principal features around London.

Detsicas 1983, 8). Sites at Brockley Hill (where Watling Street changed course) and Staines (where the Thames was crossed) might also have lain close to boundaries between London and adjacent communities.

The area crudely defined by the sites mentioned above includes most lands within a 32 km radius of London, except to the north-west where the proximity of Verulamium would have required a boundary closer to London. Without the evidence of inscriptions or historical references we cannot really know where the limits of the lands of London lay. Whatever the legal reality there can be no doubt, however, that this area around London would have been closely bound to the city by a variety of economic and social ties.

The principal symbol of Romanization in the countryside was the villa. For present purposes villas are defined as the country establishments of a gentry which followed Roman fashion. The social order that inspired the villa was structured through the town. Once the new urban élite had invested the profits of trade and government in land, and once the landed gentry had been drawn into the political and social life of the community, then villas are likely to have been built. Villas are a useful measure of the relationship between town and country, between urban society and land.

The earliest villas around London date to the period *c.* AD 80−90 and, like the better town houses of the period, were usually provided with stone foundations but often had walls of timber and clay. There were important early establishments at Lullingstone, Orpington station and Keston, and by the end of the century at Farningham and Darenth (Meates 1979; Black 1987, site 61; Girardon and Heathcote 1988; Detsicas 1983, 88−9; Black 1981). Building materials and pottery of the late first century have also been found on a small number of other sites (Black 1987, sites 59, 89 and 92). By the early second century masonry buildings, now also including bath-houses, had been built on these and other sites in the area (Black 1987, sites 38, 49 and 84). Villa development seems to have proceeded roughly in parallel with the development of town houses, although the countryside had no first-century mosaics to match those in London. Several, perhaps most, of these villas were on sites which had previously been occupied by high-status settlements (Black 1987, 22; Haselgrove 1988, 116), but without more detailed information we have no real means of knowing how the transition from British to Romano-British was achieved. New owners can find it politic to reuse traditional sites whereas long-established élites can find that changing circumstances make it convenient to move to new sites.

All of the known early villa sites within a 32 km radius of London, excluding those which lay closer to Verulamium than London, were to the south of river. This preference for the south seems to have held true throughout the Roman period. At a generous estimate there are sixty-three possible villa sites in the area; forty of these are south of the river but over 16 km from the city, with the greatest concentration in the valleys of the Cray and Darent.

The swathe of land about 16 km deep on both sides of the river, in which few villas were found, may have been dominated by public lands such as areas of communal pasture and woodland. London, to judge by animal bones found in City excavations, seems to have preferred a diet of beef with some pork but little lamb (Sheldon 1978, 33; Armitage *et al.* 1983, 30), and the town must have been surrounded by cattle; in some instances beasts destined for the table were herded to town for slaughter (Tyers 1984, 367–74). Woods were essential as a source of fuel and building material. Some of this area might first have been owned by the army; any supply base or fort in the area would have been surrounded by expropriated lands. Gifts of such lands to newly founded civic authorities would have been one of the more positive forms of assistance the provincial government could have given in the urbanization process. The Kentish villas beyond this proposed ring of public land might have been more important for arable crops (there is evidence that this was the case later in the Roman period, see Chapter 7), in addition to having served as a Roman equivalent of the stockbroker belt.

The ties between London and Kentish property are witnessed by a wooden writing tablet recently discovered in second-century reclamation dumps on the east side of the Walbrook (Fig. 19). The scratched surface

FIG. 19 A wooden writing tablet found in excavations at Throgmorton Avenue in 1986. The text, originally inscribed in a wax coating to the tablet, refers to a dispute over property in Kent.

of the wood had preserved much of the text of a legal document dated to 14 March 118 and concerning a dispute over property *in civitate Cantiacorum* (in the territory of the people of Kent), ownership of which was claimed by Lucius Iulius Betucus (Tomlin forthcoming). A further connection is suggested by Ptolemy, writing in the early second century, who thought that London lay within Kentish territory (*Geogr.* ii, 3), although he is widely considered to have been mistaken (Rivet 1964, 132, 145).

There may have been a rather different pattern of land-use in the Thames estuary. A planned landscape of rectangular boundaries might possibly have been imposed on the flatlands to north and south of the Thames early in the Roman period (Rodwell 1978, 90−3; 1979, 336; Dilke 1971, 191−3). Such organized interference in the landscape would suggest the hand of the state, and this may have been an area taken into imperial ownership and administered under the authority of the procurator. State ownership could account for both the scarcity of villas in this area and the large-scale production here of salt, a vital commodity to army and state. There may also have been extensive imperial property in the Weald, an important area of iron production. This area, rather like the Thames estuary, lay on the borders of tribal territories and could have been administered from London, although it has also been suggested that the Wealden iron industry was organized by the *Classis Britannica*, the Roman fleet, from its bases on the south coast (Cleere 1974).

Small roadside settlements, villages of modest timber buildings strung out along both sides of a principal road for between 400 m and 4 km, were also a feature of the countryside around London (Sheldon and Scharf 1978; Smith 1987). The closest to London, at Old Ford, was essentially a late Roman settlement, and will be discussed in Chapter 7. Most of the other sites were in a ring about 15−21 km out from the town; settlements have been recognized at Brentford, Brockley Hill, Enfield, Crayford and Ewell. More distant, at nearly 32 km from London, were the settlements at Springhead (around the temple site) and Staines (around the bridge and waterfront). Pre-Flavian occupation has been noted at these last two mentioned sites and at Brockley Hill (where there were important early pottery kilns); elsewhere occupation seems to have started between *c*. AD 80 and 100 and all sites appear to have been fairly busy in the early second century. It has been suggested that most of these sites grew up around official posting stations (*mutationes*) and would have serviced the needs of passing traffic (Sheldon and Scharf 1978, 63).

The economy of London

The changes of the Flavian period had a significant effect on the economy of the city. As successful campaigns took the army further away, and especially when military activity shifted from west to north, London became less vital to supply routes. At the same time, however, the city seems to have grown in importance as both a producer and consumer of Roman goods.

The merchant community of London has left little trace, although a handful of wooden writing tablets found preserved in the mud of the Walbrook give some insight into the affairs of the city. These documents, likely to date to the late first to early second centuries, seem mostly to be business contracts and declarations; their very presence is witness to the commercial interests of London. Only scraps survive: 'which money by the terms likewise of the claim shall be paid to me by Crescens or the person concerned', comes to us as the chance echo of a world of such financial agreements (Wheeler 1930, 54—5). One writing tablet mentions sales from a shop and the building of a boat (Wheeler 1930, 54—5); another, probably written from Rochester, refers to a boy who had apparently run away with some goods entrusted to his care (Turner and Skutsch 1960). The most complete text reads: 'Rufus, son of Callisunus, greetings to Eppillicus and all his fellows, I believe you know I am well, if you have made the list please send, take all good care, see that you turn that girl into cash' (Richmond 1953, 206—8). This would seem to be a letter of instruction to the manager of an estate or business, and there has been some speculation as to the meaning of the final instruction; was a debtor to be pressed or a slave girl sold? In addition to these letters there are a couple of inscriptions which may refer to people of Greek extraction, such as the tombstone to Aulus Alfidius Olussa who was apparently born at Athens (RIB 9), and the presence of a Greek community would be circumstantial evidence for the presence of a merchant community. The sum of this evidence takes us little further forward; the study of commerce remains dependent on the evidence of traded goods, and in particular on the pottery imports. The material evidence for trade in early Roman London has recently been reviewed by F. Grew, F. Pritchard and B. Richardson (in Milne 1985, 103—19) and most of the comments presented below are drawn from their text.

The Romanized tastes of London society would have created a ready market for imported luxuries. Throughout the late first and second centuries Samian remained considerably more common on sites in London than elsewhere in the south-east. New Samian imports were stored in large quantities in warehouses in the bridgehead area; hundreds of early second-century vessels were found in the Hadrianic destruction of a warehouse at Regis House and many more unused vessels were found in third-century waterfront dumps at New Fresh Wharf (Rhodes 1986, 199—203). It seems possible, however, that Samian was becoming more efficiently exported on from London. It has been noted that in the pre-Flavian period Samian accounted for over 10 per cent of the vessels on low-status sites in London, but in Chelmsford made up only 1.42 per cent of the pottery assemblage. By the Hadrianic period this figure had dropped to 7.43 per cent in London but risen to 4.3 per cent in Chelmsford, a change which perhaps reflects more developed marketing systems.

Trade in wine and oil is well represented in the archaeological record. Large ceramic amphorae which had contained wine or oil, or sometimes fish sauce or olives, are commonly found by the waterfront. Imports seem to have reached a peak in the late first and early second centuries. Very few amphorae reached the outer parts of town and it is possible that their contents had been sold by the jugful at the quayside. Some produce, mostly wine, had also been imported in wooden barrels, and empty barrels were used to line city wells. This trade also seems to have been at its peak in the late first to early second century (Wilmott 1982a, 1984). Seeds and pips found in rubbish pits and dumps inform us that fruits such as peaches, olives, figs and grapes were being brought to London; cucumber and coriander were also imported (Armitage *et al.* 1983, 29). Nine of the nineteen textile fragments found in London may have been imports. Jewellery such as bracelets of ivory, amber beads from the Baltic, and gold and emerald necklaces was also imported; and imported stone veneers were used in the decoration of some houses (although most of these were imported from elsewhere in Britain).

Many of these products were doubtless sufficiently prized to have been worth trading in any circumstances. It seems likely, however, that London still owed much of its commercial success to its ability to exploit official supply routes. The continued significance of these routes is demonstrated by a number of peculiarities in the pattern of trade. The comparative frequency of clay lamps in London and Colchester, rarely used elsewhere in the province, hints at military supply (Whittaker 1989). This is also the most likely explanation for the preference for quern- and millstones from Gaul or Germany; British quern-stones were rarely used before the third century. The products of the potteries at Brockley Hill, between London and Verulamium, continued to reach markets up and down the province with improbable success; and these and other north London kilns may have been operated by government lessees with the military market in mind (Marsh and Tyers 1978; 534; Wilkes 1981).

The needs of imperial supply were, however, beginning to change. At Richborough military occupation came to an end about AD 85, and the site had probably seen a reduction in use from as early as AD 70 (Cunliffe 1968, 234—43). Initially this may have meant that London was taking over functions served by Richborough, but it was also the first step towards the creation of new east-coast supply lines leading to bases at

York and eventually to Hadrian's Wall. These changes were of fundamental importance to London and will be given detailed attention in Chapter 5. In the shorter term, however, the port of Roman London is likely to have remained a busy place and no doubt offered considerable opportunities for employment and profit.

Although London's role as a place of transhipment may have diminished, the region may have become more productive. Surplus production from imperial estates, in particular, could have been directed towards military supply. The possible connection between the Wealden iron industry and the Roman fleet has already been noted and the salt industry of the lower Thames could also have developed around military need. This industry, which has left abundant evidence in the form of burnt clay hearths and evaporating vessels (*briquetage*), emerged in the area in the late first century and was at its peak early in the second century (Detsicas 1983, 170—1; Rodwell 1979, 160—6). It would have allowed the state to salt surplus meat and fish products from its estates — perhaps most importantly it would have allowed untanned hides to be transported in bulk. Leather was enormously important to the army; tents, uniforms, harnesses, shield coverings, shoes and a whole host of fittings were made of it. London seems to have been a significant leather-working centre and although this industry may have been primarily concerned with internal demand it may also have been buoyed up by contracts for military supply.

Large wood-lined tanks and channels have been found in second-century contexts in the upper Walbrook valley, just inside and to the north of the line of the later town wall, and there seems every possibility that this area had been extensively used in the tanning industry (DUA 1987, 193; RCHM 1928, 145—7; Heathcote 1989, 51). There is also widespread evidence for leather working from several parts of the town including the Walbrook valley, the western suburb and Southwark (Lees *et al.* 1989, 119; Wilmott forthcoming; Grimes 1968, 97; Shepherd forthcoming; Sheldon 1978, 31). Many hundreds of small leather offcuts, mostly from shoes, have now been found, especially in the reclamation dumps on the banks of the Walbrook and Thames. Tanners' marks have been recognized on some of the unused offcuts, usually close to the borders of the hides (Rhodes 1986, 89; Rhodes 1987a, 173—81). Products included shoes, cattle-hide jackets and leather breeches. The evidence suggests that there was an unusually high level of demand for leather in London and that this industry may have had an important role in the economy of the city between the late first and early third century.

Reference has already been made to the possible military influence on the success of the pottery kilns at Brockley Hill, where production concentrated on the production of specialist forms of Roman pottery (mortaria and flagons) not normally found in the repertoire of native potters. Several other sites in and around London saw pottery manufacture in this period (Marsh and Tyers 1978, 533—82). The coarse kitchen wares used in London, bowls and jars made in more traditional fabrics and styles, were mostly made at seasonal kilns such as those set up in the Highgate Wood area (Brown and Sheldon 1974). Small short-lived kiln sites were also set up in the suburbs of Flavian London. Several kilns have been noted behind ribbon development along the Roman west road, showing a similar pattern of distribution to the cemeteries (Marsden 1969; Heathcote 1989, 52). Wasters found in the upper Walbrook valley could also have come from a small suburban pottery (Marsh and Tyers 1976, 228). The products of these small sites made little impact on pottery trade within the city.

The first 15 years of the Flavian period saw vigorous suburban growth and the settlement returned broadly to the limits established before AD 60. Many previously open areas, especially in Southwark, were now built over. As previously, the larger suburbs were along Watling Street and their rapid success in the years after *c.* AD 70 is evidence for the continued importance of traffic along this route. The main streets in these suburbs were largely filled by narrow houses, often called strip buildings, in which workshops had been set behind shops, with private rooms above or behind the working areas (Perring and Roskams forthcoming; Sheldon 1978, 31; Ferretti and Graham 1978, 65–79).

Many crafts and trades were probably practised in workshops throughout the city although only rarely can specific industries be identified. Evidence for small-scale metalworking, usually iron- and bronze-working, is widespread. Smithing slag has been found in various parts of Southwark and in the Walbrook valley and a tin industry was probably based in the Walbrook area before *c.* AD 155 (Maloney 1990; Wilmott forthcoming; Sheldon 1978, 31; Jones 1983, 49–59). Rather more exotic is the evidence for gold-working; parts of crucibles used for refining gold were found with lids and sealings in pits containing late Flavian pottery near Suffolk Lane (Marsden 1975, 9–12). Some evidence for gold-working has also been found in Southwark (Sheldon 1978, 31). Tools found in the Walbrook – including tongs, punches, hammers, an anvil and a large furnace bar – further testify to the craft workshops of London. Several sites have also provided evidence for glass-making, mostly in the form of waste glass and glass-coated burnt clay. An important collection of glass-working debris, including part of a tank furnace, was found at 55–61 Moorgate and has provisionally been dated to the period AD 140–60 (Richardson 1988, 386). Glass-working waste has also been found on several other sites in the upper Walbrook valley (Maloney 1990) and parts of furnace lining, pot metal, droplets, cuttings and wastes were found beneath the internal rampart of the city wall in excavations at the Tower; it is probable that there had been a second-century glass-blowing workshop in this area (Bayley and Shepherd 1985, 72–3). The evidence from these and other sites suggests that imported cullet was probably

FIG. 20   Bread ovens found in a building to the east of the Flavian forum.

used rather than local sand, and that the industry flourished between the late first and early third century.

Most of the buildings and industries briefly considered above are likely to have been engaged in supplying and servicing the needs of the large urban population. This was indisputably the case for another principal trade of the city – baking. Baking, like tanning, was one of the more important urban industries of the Roman world, and evidence for milling and baking is abundant in the area around the London forum. Six circular bread ovens were found in a late first-century timber building opposite the south-east corner of the forum (Fig. 20) and two others in a contemporary building at 22–23 Birchin Lane; burnt grain was also found at Birchin Lane (Philp 1977, 22–3; Richardson 1988, 382). Excavations at Bucklersbury House in Walbrook Street showed that the Walbrook here had been funnelled into a narrow channel, a large millstone of German lava lay near by, and it has been suggested that this was the site of a watermill (Marsden 1980, 72). A donkey-mill, represented by a large hour-glass-shaped millstone, was found in Prince's Street near the

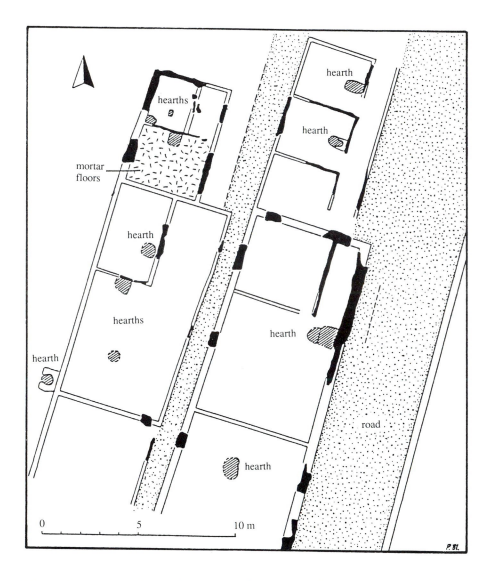

FIG. 21   Plan of the early second-century strip buildings found in the excavations at Newgate Street (after Bentley in Perring and Roskams).

Walbrook, and further discoveries of millstones and grain have been made in the area west towards Cheapside (Shepherd 1987). The evidence concentrates in the area of the forum. The remains of three black rats were found in the fills of a mid third-century well to the south of the forum, at 5−12 Fenchurch Street, and might hint that grain had been stored near by (Armitage *et al.* 1984, 375−82).

The building industry would have kept a horde of craftsmen and labourers employed. This, along with the work generated by the activities of the port, was one of the more important ways in which profits from the conquest of Britain were able to enter the local economy. A related element of the contemporary economy is likely to have been the property market. It is probable that the rented sector of the housing market provided for all but a small proportion of the urban population in antiquity (Casey 1985, 43). London's comparatively large urban population may have encouraged many landowners to become landlords and several houses of *c.* AD 100 could have been designed for multiple occupancy. A row of narrow single-storey buildings, separated by narrow alleys, were squeezed close together behind the early forum. These were demolished to make way for the larger second-century forum and the remains of several were studied in the excavations at Leadenhall Court (Brigham *et al.* 1987, 19). Typically the houses comprised a row of rooms 4 m square, each with a small hearth. It is possible that these were simple one-roomed lodgings; bed-sitters for working men. Since these buildings lay in an area later used for public buildings it is just possible that they had always been on public property and had provided the city with rents; several other buildings around the early forum, such as the bakehouse to the southeast, could have done the same.

Rooms for rent may also have been set at the back of one of the workshops found in excavations off Newgate Street; a row of three small square rooms, each with its fireplace, were set off a corridor (Fig. 21) (Perring and Roskams forthcoming). This corridor was reached by a side entrance and there was no evident communication between these rooms and the rest of the building. Identical rows of self-contained rooms are found attached to some houses in Italy where they accommodated slaves.

A house discovered at Watling Court might have offered a better class of lodging (Fig. 22). The reconstructed plan of this building hints that it may have been divided into three units of four to six rooms; these could have been three apartments. This house was probably in the same property as the building with the early mosaic floors (*see* above, page 40), and had perhaps provided the veteran we suppose to have lived here with income (Perring and Roskams forthcoming).

Milne has suggested that since much of the imported material found in London was of a luxury character 'it may have been brought in primarily to satisfy the needs of the richer strata of Romano-British citizens, many of whom lived in London. The expanding town itself may therefore have been the main magnet, attracting quantities of exotic material for sale and consumption within its boundaries' (Milne 1985, 149). This argument has a certain amount of truth but it is difficult to believe that the thriving economy of the late first to early second century could have been sustained on the basis of internal demand alone.

The economy of the Flavian city seems to have had several very great advantages. Firstly, London seems to have remained an important centre for military supply during the earlier stages of the campaigns in northern Britain; the city must have had some opportunity to profit from military contracts and retained some advantage from subsidized trade links with Germany and Gaul. The spoils of conquest, such as they were, are also likely to have trickled back through London since this was where the principal agent of conquest, the provincial government, was based. Secondly, the city received a massive injection of capital on public building projects; some of the capital for these projects may have been local, some may not, but the important point is that resources which in the pre-Flavian period had perhaps been transferred out of the province, or hoarded, were being poured into the local economy. Thirdly, markets for Roman imports and Roman skills, best supplied through London, were now becoming more highly developed as the process of the Romanization of British society began in earnest. Lastly, and here we can agree fully with Milne, the city as a busy centre of government for both province and territory had acquired a wealthy resident élite who offered an attractively rich and compact market for merchants of luxury goods and purveyors of urban services. With all of these factors acting in its favour it is not surprising that London prospered.

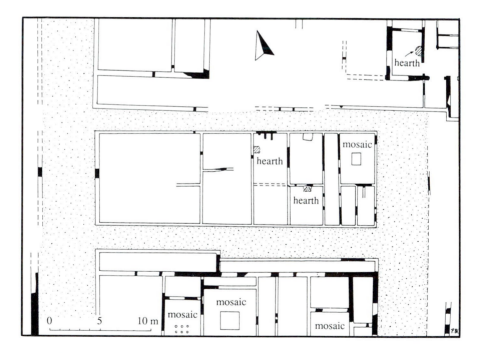

FIG. 22 Plan of first-century town houses at Watling Court (after Bentley in Perring and Roskams). The earlier house, where the fragment of the military diploma and the early mosaics were found, is to the south; the building in the centre of the site was probably in the same property and may have been divided into apartments. The building in the north-east corner of the site had a second storey.

4 The city in its prime (*c.* AD 100−150)

Public buildings

By the end of the first century London had already acquired most of the public buildings it would have needed but this did little to slow the pace of construction. The building programme continued vigorously into the second century, although most later works were concerned with enlarging or replacing earlier structures. London seems to have found its earliest public buildings were inadequate; perhaps it had outgrown them, perhaps the city had been promoted in status (as from *municipium* to *colonia*), or perhaps the habit of building was difficult to break. After over two decades of continuous construction work there might well have been a strong lobby of interest pressing the city to find new building projects.

The most imposing of these projects was the complete reconstruction of the forum (Fig. 23). The evidence for the second forum was recently reviewed by Peter Marsden (Marsden 1987), and subsequent work at Leadenhall Court, by a team led by Gustav Milne, has added important detail. Marsden suggests a construction date of *c.* AD 100 for the second forum, although the more recent investigations suggest that construction work may still have been in progress as late as AD 130 (Brigham 1990). The construction process was both protracted and complicated, and it seems that the new forum was built around the Flavian one which remained standing until a late stage in the building process. The forum covered an area 166 by 167 m and the new basilica measured 52.5 by 167 m. This had a nave flanked by side aisles with an apsidal-ended tribunal at the east end. A further range of rooms was added alongside the northern aisle. Discoveries at Leadenhall Court suggest that several of the features described by Marsden may not have been part of the original construction; the arcading between the nave and northern aisle perhaps dates to a rebuilding of the early second century and the southern aisle may also have been added at this time (Brigham 1990). Work at Whittington Avenue has shown that the outer portico on the east side of the forum, which had a tile floor, was also a later addition (G. Brown, personal communication) (Fig. 24).

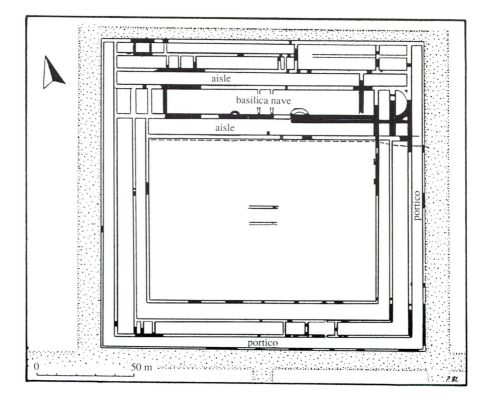

FIG. 23 A reconstruction of the plan of the Trajanic—Hadrianic forum (after Marsden). The evidence is presented in a somewhat simplified form and the original building may have been slightly less regular in appearance.

The courtyard to the south of the basilica was enclosed by ranges of rooms and porticoes and contained a structure which Marsden suggests might have been a pool. This feature was 7.43 m wide but, since its floor was set at a higher level than some of the surrounding courtyard surfaces, may have been part of a small building or cross passage rather than a pool (Marsden 1987, Fig. 55; T. Brigham, personal communication). Foundations on the east side of the forum suggest that there may have been side entrances, others to the south may have supported statues. The scale of this new forum was most impressive. The complex was the largest in Britain, although smaller than that at Trier, and the basilica, which was about the length of St Paul's, was the largest in the north-west provinces.

The baths on Huggin Hill were also comprehensively restructured in the early second century, probably *c.* AD 120, although many of the earlier elements were retained (Marsden 1976). The principal effect of a fairly complicated series of alterations was to create a new range of rooms over what might originally have been the building forecourt. The cold rooms originally at the east end of the building were now in its middle.

FIG. 24 Part of the herringbone tile floor of the portico east of the forum basilica, as found in recent excavations at Whittington Avenue.

To the west a second hot room was set on the north side of the building, this had an apsidal end and measured 8.2 by *c.* 11 m. To the east a new range of rooms had been built; a third hot room, at the far end of this range, measured 8.81 by 15.95 m with an apsidal end. The interior of the building had been decorated by imported marbles, fragments of which were found in its ruins. The new arrangement made the fullest possible use of a rather awkward terrace site.

Further traces of public buildings have been found to the north-west of the baths (Marsden 1976, 49–51). Two parallel walls, 9.32–9.85 m apart, have been recorded along Knightrider Street (Fig. 25). The northern wall was at least 115 m long and stood above ground level, and it must have enclosed a precinct or open space of some kind. It had cut into a pit with late first-century pot and elsewhere pottery of the third to fourth century had been dumped to its side. It is possible that some of the elements recorded in this area, including the wall to the south, might have been added to the building complex in a later phase (Williams forthcoming). Extensive gravel surfaces and several quarry pits have been noted on sites to the north and a 21 m long masonry wall set perpendicular to Knightrider Street was seen at Sermon Lane (Merrifield 1965, sites 81–84; Marsden 1968, 2–3). Two recent studies have suggested that this might have been the site of a circus (Humphrey 1986, 431; Fuentes 1986, 144–7). Circuses were important sites for festivals and sports in early Roman cities. No other Romano-British circus is known but London, because of its size and importance, might well have had one. The plan of the Knightrider Street walls, especially a curved wall line at the east end, does not, however, make a very convincing case for this having been its site.

Alternatively, the Knightrider Street walls might have enclosed a temple precinct. The small temple adjacent to the forum had been cleared away in the early second-century rebuilding and a religious complex ought to have been built elsewhere by this date. Temples in other towns in south-

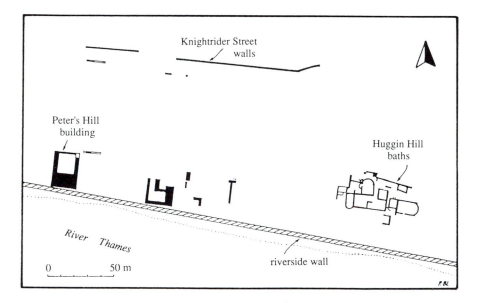

FIG. 25   Plan of the main walls and buildings found in the south-west corner of the city (based on drawings by Marsden and Williams). The Huggin Hill baths had been demolished before the monumental foundations, perhaps part of a palace or temple complex, were built at Peter's Hill.

east Britain were set in extensive gravelled precincts and there are few other parts of London where a large temple site could have totally avoided detection. Roman town planners when faced with a hilly site were wont to place the gods on one hill to overlook the magistrates on another; Ludgate Hill is slightly higher than Cornhill.

This speculation is given some support by the fact that the slopes below the Knightrider Street walls may later have been occupied by a religious precinct; indeed it can be suggested that the baths at Huggin Hill had been attached to such a precinct (Williams forthcoming; Merrifield 1980). A dump of marble veneers found beneath a late third-century building excavated at Peter's Hill included material of a much higher standard than anything seen associated with the Huggin Hill baths and is likely to have come from another public building in the area. Some of the marbles used (as Italian Carrara) were rarely used after the second century whereas some other types (as the black and white 'Aquitaine' marble) were not usually used before the third century (Pritchard 1988, 187). This dump might therefore have come from the demolition of a first- or second-century building which had been extensively refurbished in the third century. Foundations recorded by Peter Marsden at the site of the Salvation Army Headquarters, adjacent to the Peter's Hill site, might have been part of this building complex (Marsden 1967). Immense Roman walls noted in the area above Huggin Hill might also have been associated with public buildings in the area (Merrifield 1965, sites 103 and 104).

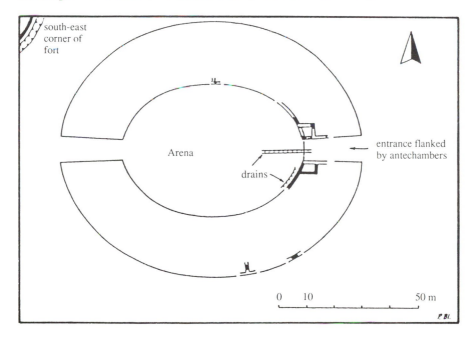

FIG. 26 Plan of the amphitheatre (after Welman).

FIG. 27 The amphitheatre entrance, with flanking side chambers, and timber-lined drain found in excavations at Guildhall Yard. The larger foundations are modern.

One of the buildings that might have been found hereabouts is the theatre. London need not necessarily have had a theatre, it could have relied exclusively on the amphitheatre, but such buildings were commonly attached to religious complexes. Fuentes has suggested that this may have been found at St Andrew's Hill although recent excavations seem to suggest that most of the topographical elements here were medieval in origin (Fuentes 1986, 144–7; Heathcote 1989, 47).

One of the more exciting discoveries of recent years was the Roman amphitheatre (Heathcote 1989, 50) (Figs 26 and 27). A curved stone wall, 1 m wide, enclosed an oval gravel floored arena 62 by 44 m, and retained earth banks which would have supported tiers of wooden seats. The entrance way was a 7 m wide tunnel flanked by two small chambers which are likely to have been shrines to the goddess of retribution, Nemesis. A large wooden drain crossed the arena and gutter drains followed the inside of the retaining wall. The external dimensions of the stadium can be reconstructed as 130 by 110 m which make it the largest known from Roman Britain. Provisional results from the study of the timbers used in this building suggest it to have been built *c.* 120 although it may possibly have replaced an earlier amphitheatre on the same site.

A lump of very hard masonry noted in building works at Goldsmiths' Hall, to the south-west of the amphitheatre, might just conceivably have been part of a temple podium or shrine. An altar from this site, probably of the second century, depicted a hunter or huntress, perhaps Diana or Atys (Toynbee 1962, 152).

The building discovered at 15–23 Southwark Street and tentatively identified as a *mansio* was also rebuilt during the second century. It is not clear whether or not it retained its earlier function, although the presence of an early hypocaust floor demonstrates the high status of the building (Beard and Cowan 1988, 380). This floor was unusual both for being set within a clay-walled building and for the use of circular supports (Fig. 28). These are perhaps early features and suggest that the building might have been rebuilt in the earlier part of the century.

Early in the second century a large and very luxurious building was built in a prominent position on the south bank of the Thames (Yule 1989, 33–5) (Fig. 29). In the recent excavations at Winchester Palace parts of seven rooms, five heated by hypocaust floors, were found over the levelled remains of the stone building described on page 34. In one of the rooms a richly painted lunette had fallen on to the floor (Fig. 30). This had originally shown a winged Cupid at the centre of an elaborate framework of flimsy pavilions (Ling 1989). The exceptional quality of the painting is shown by the use of luxury materials such as red cinnabar and gold leaf (at the time of its discovery only one other building of Roman Britain was known to have had gold leaf in its wall paintings), and it bears comparison with contemporary work in Italy. A mosaic with coloured

FIG. 28   A hypocaust floor in a clay-walled building found at 15−23 Southwark High Street.

geometric patterns had probably been on the floor of the room. This building had the aspect of a palatial suburban villa although some features suggest that it may have been a public building. It has already been noted that the scale and quality of the earlier building on the site were such as to hint at public ownership, and it may also be significant that this site had probably remained in occupation from the second to fourth centuries; such longevity was unusual in Southwark and possibly more common in public buildings than private ones. A third-century inscription from the site listed soldiers, and Brian Yule has suggested on the basis of a similar inscription from York that the troops had a base, perhaps a guild head-quarters, in the area (Yule 1989, 35). This may have been the palace of a high-ranking imperial official.

Towards the middle of the second century the waterfront terrace on the north bank of the Thames was significantly enlarged by extending timber quays up to 25 m further out over the foreshore (Milne 1985). The eastern part of this new waterfront, excavated at the Custom House, was unlikely to have been built before AD 145 (Hillam *et al.* 1984), but a date of *c.* AD 150 would fit the available evidence in all areas (an earlier date than first thought likely, Tatton-Brown 1974). The storage buildings at

FIG. 29 A general view of the suburban villa found on the banks of the Thames at the Winchester Palace site; traces of a hypocaust floor can be seen in the foreground.

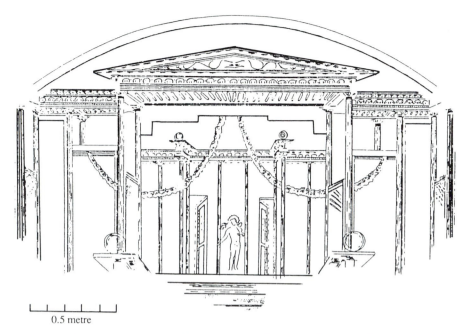

0.5 metre

FIG. 30   A drawing of the painted lunette found at Winchester Palace (by S. A. Mackenna).

Pudding Lane were left some distance behind the waterfront and were probably converted into shops at this time (Milne 1985, 30). The waterfront advance was not dictated by the structural decay of the earlier quays, nor would it have offered any significant advantage to the boatmen; the extensions are most likely to have been designed to win land.

These new quays had engulfed the pier base thought likely to have supported the bridge over the Thames and it is therefore possible that a new bridge was also built (Milne 1985, 54). A lead *defixio* found on the Thames foreshore is addressed to Metunus (Neptune) and its presence has given rise to the suggestion that there had been a shrine to Neptune by the bridge (Hassall and Tomlin 1987, 360–3).

The city enlarged

The early second century saw ambitious programmes of reclamation and drainage in the upper Walbrook valley. This area has been the subject of a detailed study by Cathy Maloney who concludes that a new road system was laid out *c.* AD 120 after initial and not wholly successful attempts to drain the marshier parts of the area in the late first century (Fig. 31) (Maloney 1990). The new street grid filled the area between the Walbrook and the Cripplegate fort to the north of the pre-Flavian road at 24–25 Ironmonger Lane (Fig. 32) (Shepherd 1987). The northern limit of this new part of the town has not yet been identified but might have been to the north of the later city wall. Occupation, especially buildings and features associated with the tanning industry, had clearly extended for

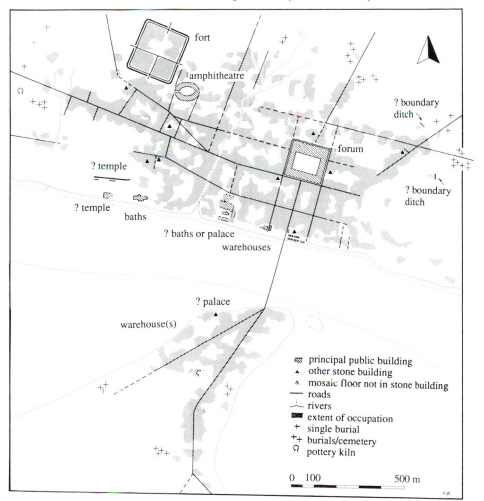

FIG. 31 Trajanic–Hadrianic London, showing the extent of development in *c.* AD 130.

FIG. 32   Part of one of the streets laid out in the upper Walbrook valley, at Copthall Avenue, in the early second century. The compact gravel surfaces were laid over a bank of turves set on a brushwood raft.

some 50–100 m north of the later city wall and sites around Finsbury Circus have revealed traces of road surfaces and occupation debris (Heathcote 1989, 49, 51). It is likely, however, that the northernmost part of this area was never formally incorporated into the city. Cremation urns, one with a coin of Antoninus Pius (AD 138–61), have been found just inside the line of the later city wall at Bishopsgate which strongly suggests that the early second-century boundary was slightly to the south of the later city wall (RCHM 1928, pl. 55).

Suburbs may, for the first time, have extended north of the city along Bishopsgate; traces of second-century occupation have been recorded to the north of Liverpool Street station, at Stothard Place, although some areas between here and the city proper are likely to have remained open (DUA 1987, 193).

Further to the east it seems probable that the line of the second-century boundary was followed by the city wall. At Duke's Place a shallow ditch 0.6 m deep and over 4 m wide, with second-century fills, predicted the line of the city wall (Maloney 1979). This ditch had cut through layers which sealed the remains of a timber building, perhaps Flavian, which suggests that this particular boundary was not established much before the beginning of the second century. Further traces of a pre-wall ditch have been noted on at least three nearby sites (Merrifield 1965, site 336; Marsden 1980, 46 note 16; Maloney 1983, 97).

The western boundary of the city presents a more complicated problem. The pattern of burials might indicate that the city boundary had reached its *c.* AD 200 location sometime in the middle or later second century but earlier in the century it may still have been some distance to the east (Maloney 1983, 97). A watercourse noted in this area, and in part earlier than the city wall, seems to have been canalized; perhaps it had been re-directed during alterations to the city boundary. This watercourse, the evidence for which has recently been reviewed by David Bentley, was up to 21.34 m across and in the north consisted of two separate channels (Bentley 1987; Norman and Reader 1912, 274—84). The eastern of these channels was bounded by a 2.4 m thick wall. The lower observations referred to by Bentley contained medieval fills, and might possibly relate to a medieval castle, Montfichet's tower, rather than the Roman feature (see Heathcote 1989, 47).

Buildings have been noted outside the line of the city wall on the western side of the city, and others were disturbed during the construction of the wall (Bentley and Pritchard 1982; DUA 1987, 28, 138; Grimes 1968, 128ff; RCHM 1928, 147; Merrifield 1983, 133; Norman and Reader 1912, 280). Most were second and third century in date and all contained high-quality floors. Some may have been suburban villas.

The sum of this evidence is that the city had grown to cover an area equivalent to that enclosed by the city wall of *c.* AD 200 (about 125 ha), by the mid second century, although some of this space may still have been considered suburban. The suburb south of the river is estimated to have been at its greatest extent in the late first to early second centuries, and this perhaps covered some 13 ha (Sheldon 1978, 16). Not all of the space within the city was, however, built over; the corners in particular seem to have been little used. Excavations at Peter's Hill have shown the south-west corner to have been unused and there were few buildings in a low-lying area, probably a shallow valley, in the south-east corner of the later walled area (Williams forthcoming; Bentley 1984). Investigations in this eastern valley, at Rangoon Street, have shown that ditch systems were laid out in the early Flavian period. These were perhaps animal enclosures or field boundaries (Bowler 1983, 13—19).

Elsewhere the city was very crowded. This was evident not only in the crowded jostle of shops and houses along the main streets, or in the tightly packed tenements out of sight behind the forum, but also in the better residential areas. A striking aspect of the Watling Court site was the absence of open space around what were some of the best town houses of the period (Fig. 22) (Perring and Roskams forthcoming). Parts of six or more buildings divided by narrow alleyways were found but there was no green space at all. One of the buildings at Watling Court had probably had an upper floor, and a mosaic appeared to have collapsed from an upper room. In Roman houses upper floors were usually lesser floors; the best rooms, the dining rooms and halls, were usually on the ground floor. Only in densely populated towns, such as Ostia, was space at such a premium that reception rooms were commonly placed in upper floors. London was no Ostia, indeed the vast majority of its buildings were single storey, but it is clear that London was a very crowded place *c.* AD 100. Comparison is difficult but it was quite possibly twice as populous as the city destroyed in AD 60.

The larger city had larger cemeteries. Cemeteries close to the principal points of entry into town, but not exclusively along roads, had been established by the early second century. The principal burial areas were to the north-west of Newgate (around Smithfield), north-west of Bishopsgate (to Finsbury Circus), south-east of Aldgate, and around the fringes of Southwark (Bentley and Pritchard 1982; Evans and Pierpoint 1986; Dean and Hammerson 1980; Dean 1981). It seems likely that the cemeteries outside Bishopsgate and Aldgate only became popular *c.* AD 120, perhaps because of the changes to the city boundaries effected at about this time. There were also a number of individual burials along the main roads into the city. These are most evident along Holborn and the westernmost yet reported was found with early Flavian coins at Endell Street, over 1.5 km from the city wall. This emphasis indicates that the road west towards Watling Street was perceived to be the most important route into town.

Cremation continued to be the most popular burial rite in the second century, to become rare during the third, although there were also some inhumations of this period. Pits in which the cremations took place have been found in the cemeteries at West Tenter Street and Mansell Street (Richardson 1985, 63–7). The cremated remains were buried in a variety of containers: pots, amphorae, lead urns, tile cists and possibly wooden casks are known to have been used (Fig. 33) (Whytehead 1986, 49). Little evidence for above-ground structures has been found although some walls of a masonry structure discovered at Tenter Street, with marble veneer in the destruction debris, are likely to have been part of a mausoleum.

Some of the dead had been treated in a rather peculiar way. Skulls, mostly of young to middle-aged men, had been thrown into the Walbrook and other wet places during the first and second centuries. The practice, which seems to have had pre-Roman origins, continued until at least the middle of the second century (Bradley and Gordon 1988, 503–9; Maloney 1990). The missing bodies had probably been cremated in the normal way. In a thorough examination of the evidence then available Geoff Marsh and Barbara West concluded that about half the skulls had been exposed for some time before deposition, and that the whole business was linked to the continued practice of Celtic head-cults (Marsh and West 1981, 86–101).

FIG. 33 A tile-lined cist containing a broken cremation urn, as found in excavations at Barnard's Inn, Holborn in 1988.

The fires of London

London suffered a number of fires in the Roman period; some seem to have been fairly localized affairs, others caused enormous destruction. Evidence of burning on some sites west of the Walbrook has been tentatively identified as early Flavian, although it is perhaps more probable that these represent a further area of destruction of AD 60 (Perring and Roskams forthcoming). There is clear evidence of a late Flavian fire to the south of the forum; this was first recognized by Roskams and Watson (1981) and has been confirmed by stratigraphic excavation at 27–30 Lime Street (Williams in preparation; see also Hammer 1987, 7–8; Bateman 1986, 237).

The greatest of London's Roman fires was the Hadrianic fire, evidence for which is found in most city excavations (Dunning 1945; Roskams and Watson 1981). The fire is best dated from the evidence of a Samian warehouse found at Regis House; the burnt debris here was 1.2 m thick, and contained fragments of at least 600 newly imported vessels which date the fire to AD 120–25 (Marsh 1981). Evidence for this fire has been clearly identified to the south of the forum and along most of the road to Newgate, extending as far along this street as we know there to have been houses. Elsewhere the evidence is patchier. The fire had clearly not reached the upper Walbrook valley, which may not yet have been densely occupied and was in any case abundantly supplied with running water; and only touched the Thames at a couple of points near the bridge (Milne 1985, 29). The forum basilica was not burnt and the areas to its north and east may also have been little damaged, although Hadrianic destruction seems probable immediately to the east of the forum at Lime Street (Williams in preparation). Burnt debris has also been noted at several sites along the roads leading north and east (Bishopsgate and Fenchurch Street) and it is possible that the fire had followed the areas of more densely packed roadside housing. It has not yet been conclusively demonstrated that any of these recorded instances of fire destruction date to the Hadrianic period and there are a number of sites along these streets apparently unaffected by the fire.

Most houses and shops were empty when disaster struck. Only at Regis House were large quantities of goods evidently destroyed and it is tempting to suggest that the fire had started in this quayside area, and been taken west by the wind. This would explain why destruction was so comprehensive along Newgate Street and how it was possible to deflect the fire from the forum and the public buildings along the riverside. Fires have been noted on several other second-century sites in the London region; and although it can be argued that these were connected with disorders of the period there is no proof of this (Sheldon and Scharf 1978, 66; Sheldon 1975). The fact that none of the principal public buildings is known to have been burnt in the Hadrianic fire of London makes it unlikely that this had been a case of civil insurrection; it was probably a 'natural' disaster similar to the fire of 1666.

In most areas post-fire recovery was prompt, and although there are some parts where redevelopment was delayed or on a reduced scale, as at Watling Court and 27−30 Lime Street; these were compensated for by areas of new occupation in the upper Walbrook valley. It is perhaps significant that prime commercial sites, such as that in Newgate Street, were redeveloped almost immediately (Perring and Roskams forthcoming; Williams in preparation).

The wealth of London

The imported luxuries and new public amenities testify to a fast improving lifestyle for those Roman Londoners able to enjoy the city to the full. The early to mid second century saw a significant proportion of this prosperity translated into domestic architecture. Buildings were still predominantly of timber and unfired clay, but the quality of construction and internal decoration improved notably. Mosaics were more common in the mid second century than previously, and wall veneers of continental marbles, first used in buildings of the late first century, are found with greater frequency in deposits of this date (Pritchard 1988, 186). It is also possible that some houses were now equipped with private baths. At Pudding Lane a masonry and tile walled building put up in the rearrangement of the area after the Hadrianic fire contained a small bath-block with a mosaic-lined plunge bath and a room with a latrine set over a tile-lined drain (Fig. 34) (Building 6, Milne 1985, 140). Milne suggests that the baths were perhaps larger than would have been needed in a private house. He fancies that this may have been the site of an inn, but he perhaps underestimates the importance attached to lavish hospitality in the Roman world; private baths would have been open to a wide circle of friends and clients.

Another bath-block was found just off Cheapside (Marsden 1976). This flint and mortar building measured 21.6 by 13.7 m and in its earliest phase consisted of three principal rooms: a cold, warm and hot room. The cold room had a herring-bone tile pavement and a cold bath on one side. Hypocaust floors were laid in the other rooms and the hot room, which measured 4.9 by 6 m, had an apse at one end and a hot bath to one side. No datable finds were recovered from the building's construction levels. New floors were laid in most of the rooms during later refurbishment, and a single pottery sherd of the late first or early second century was found in these levels. Finds suggest that the building had been destroyed in the late second or third century. Marsden has suggested that the baths

FIG. 34   A latrine and part of a mosaic floor in the mid second-century town house or inn, built close to the waterfront at Pudding Lane.

were first built in the first century but a later date is also possible. The building seems to have been untouched by the Hadrianic fire, even though destruction debris lay thick on all surrounding sites and the fire had come to within 3 or 4 m of the building. It might have been built in the period of post-fire reconstruction. The modest scale of the baths suggests that they were more probably private than public, perhaps behind a town house set against Newgate Street; stone walls and tessellated pavements were noted over the Hadrianic fire debris in this area. Private baths became more common later in the Roman period, and those at Pudding Lane and Cheapside are already notably early if put up shortly after AD 125.

Other masonry buildings erected after the Hadrianic fire have been found at Watling Court, Gateway House, 3–5 Bishopsgate, and possibly also at Paternoster Square and Milk Street (Perring and Roskams forthcoming; Shepherd 1986, 1987; Milne *et al.* 1984). Larger and better decorated houses were also evident in Verulamium from the mid second century (Frere 1983b, 237–41), and even small towns around London, such as Staines, may have seen similar changes (Crouch and Shanks 1984, 3). The process of improvement was not restricted to the houses of the very rich; shops and workshops showed increasing architectural pretension in the early second century. Those excavated at Newgate Street had been rebuilt to have reception rooms with painted walls and cement floors. These modest shops were as well decorated as the very best houses of *c.* AD 60; the city had come a long way by the early second century.

5 The city in contraction (*c.* AD 150–200)

Evidence for contraction

It has long been suspected that 'Londinium, a very flourishing town at the beginning of the 2nd century, may have afterwards dwindled very markedly in size' (Waddington 1930, 68–9). More recently the argument for a decline in the London settlement has been restated by Harvey Sheldon with particular reference to results from excavations in Southwark (Sheldon 1975, 278–84). Latest work on the northern side of the river seems to confirm his case; deposits of the century prior to *c.* AD 150 are two to three times as common as those of the following century (Vince 1987, Fig. 102).

Summary reports of recently excavated domestic sites, where cellars had not completely removed later Roman levels, record late first- to mid second-century occupation in thirty-seven cases but only fourteen sites where there were buildings of the third or fourth century; in most cases the early buildings were covered by dark earth. Studies of pits and wells found in London and Southwark have given similar results; in all cases features of the first third of the Roman period are two to three times as common as those of the later period (Marsden 1980, 148, 213; Yule 1982, 246; Wilmott 1982a). Most of this evidence concerns building density, and since later houses were frequently larger than early ones the decline in building numbers must have been even more marked. These observations point towards a drastic reduction in the population of London.

The scale of change seems so considerable that the evidence must be questioned. Third-century deposits can often be hard to date; imports of Samian and coin were much reduced in the late second century and as a consequence older material remained longer in circulation. It has been suggested that many buildings thought to date to the second century might therefore have been occupied into the third century (Morris 1975, 343–4). Some imported pottery did, however, come to London during this period, and buildings and layers of the late second and early third centuries are generally recognizable. More to the point is the fact that most of the early second-century buildings of London were built of timber and clay and needed frequent repair and reconstruction. On many sites buildings erected immediately after the Hadrianic fire were never repaired or replaced, and it is difficult to imagine that they could still have been in use at the end of the century.

Further confusion is caused by the fact that on some sites the relevant levels had been disturbed. It can be argued that there was no contraction at all, that the later Roman buildings had been completely dug away at a later date (Smith 1987, 101). On two recently excavated sites, at Foster Lane and St Alban's House, traces of late second- to early third-century buildings only survived where floors had slumped into earlier pits; elsewhere the occupation layers of this phase had been destroyed later in the Roman period (Chitwood and Hill 1987; Blair 1983). At Newgate Street the remains of the final building phase were poorly preserved and had been contaminated by several late third-century finds. The site had obviously been disturbed but the evidence of the finds, of the later pits and intrusive features, and of the stratigraphy slumped into earlier features clearly indicated that it had remained unoccupied between the destruction of buildings *c.* AD 140/60 and the disturbance of the site in the late third century (Perring and Roskams forthcoming). The same can be argued for all sites where late Roman disturbance has been identified; root and worm action beneath the dark earth may have destroyed some surfaces but it is unlikely that more than one or two phases of timber buildings were affected. Such disturbance cannot account for the paucity of later Roman pits, wells and foundations. It is also significant that on several sites the walls of the latest buildings had been spread over the site rather than robbed for reuse; this suggests that demolition had preceded abandonment rather than reconstruction. At 88 Borough High Street the deliberate demolition of a clay-walled structure was dated *c.* AD 150–70; and two pits of *c.* AD 190–220 were later dug into the demolition debris (Yule 1982, 248; 1988, 79). At Well Court the buildings were flattened off by the end of the century, and a cellar filled with building debris. At Milk Street although there was no clear evidence of a destruction horizon dark earth laid over the site had closely followed the uneven contours of the buildings demolished *c.* AD 160 (Perring and Roskams forthcoming).

The evidence from both sides of the river suggests that in most cases desertion occurred between AD 150 and 200. Roadside sites furthest from the city centre seem to have been the first to suffer, and for that reason the evidence for contraction seems more marked in Southwark and the western suburb, but by the end of the century a wide range of sites had been affected. The demolition of buildings with mosaic floors at Milk Street, and of the baths near Cheapside (Marsden 1976), shows that the changes of this period were not restricted to the poorer suburbs; indeed dark earth seems to have covered stone buildings with tessellated floors in the very centre of town (as at Clement's Lane, Evans and James 1983, 26). In general the evidence from London is clear and affects all parts of the settlement: in the decades around AD 100 there were more buildings than open spaces, but from *c.* AD 200 onwards the reverse was true. The order of change suggested by the evidence is simply staggering; it is difficult to escape the conclusion that a large part of the city, perhaps as much as two-thirds, had somehow vanished.

Dark earth

Sooner or later most of Roman London was buried beneath layers of dark earth. These could be anything up to 1.5 m thick, and can be dated as early as the late second century or as late as the sixteenth. The dark earth appears to have been a garden soil; earth enriched by compost, street sweepings or 'night soil' in order to make it more suitable for gardening (Sheldon 1978, 40). In some cases thick dumps of dark earth had been tipped on to site (tip lines were seen at Newgate Street and at Milk Street the latest Roman levels were sufficiently well preserved for it to be suggested that they had been deeply buried by a single phase dump). It seems likely, however, that in most cases the dark earth had been intro-

FIG. 35 The levelled remains of second-century buildings at Newgate Street. The stake-holes were filled and covered by dark earth and were perhaps associated with late Roman gardening activity on the site.

duced in stages. There are sites where pits and post-holes have been found between identical and virtually indistinguishable layers of dark earth, as at 201–211 Borough High Street and Well Court (Sheldon 1978, 40; Perring and Roskams, forthcoming). Perhaps in some cases the dark earth had been so thoroughly dug over, or extensively disturbed by roots or worms, that layer distinctions were hard to identify. The damage to the late second-century layers at Foster Lane, St Alban's House and Newgate Street might have happened in such a mixing process. It seems unlikely that any of these sites had been ploughed since no furrows were found cutting into the disturbed buildings, but spade marks have been noted at Warwick Square (Marsden 1980, 67). On several sites, including Newgate Street, the latest Roman levels were pock-marked by a series of small holes cut from beneath or within the dark earth (Fig. 35). Many were stake-holes and some might have been root-holes; similar holes have been found in the gardens of Pompeii (Jashemski 1979).

At Milk Street the finds in the dark earth were carefully plotted in order to see if earlier ones lay to the bottom of the layer; this was not the case and it was either a single phase dump or had been thoroughly mixed at a later date. On most city sites the dark earth contains late Roman material, often of the late third to early fourth century. Either dark earth was rarely laid until this date or earlier dark earth was usually mixed with later material. Since late second-century dark earth has been recognized on sites where it was protected beneath the floors of late Roman buildings, as at Lombard Street and at 11 Ironmonger Lane, the second of these possibilities seems the more likely (Frere 1988, 463; Dawe and Oswald 1952; Shepherd 1987).

Only later mixing can easily account for the absence of early layers of soil at Rangoon Street. The open land here was used differently after the later second century; the Flavian ditch systems were maintained into the mid second century, but the latest ditches were filled *c.* AD 140–60/70 and the site sealed by a layer of dark earth with late third- to fourth-century finds. Perhaps livestock enclosures had given way to fields or gardens. It is significant that the only 'soil' on this site appeared to be the single layer of late Roman dark earth. This was probably not a single dump but an accumulation built up over two or three centuries of cultivation (Bowler 1983, 13).

Dark earth suggests gardening, and the character of the dark earth suggests that different parts of the city were made into gardens at different times and in different ways. This is only to be expected, and no single explanation works for all dark earth sites. There are, however, several general conclusions which can be drawn. It seems likely that dark earth was laid over the levelled sites of buildings when areas were deliberately turned over to cultivation. This process had started by the end of the second century and it is quite possible that most sites cleared of buildings soon became gardens. Once under cultivation further organic materials, including household rubbish, were mixed into the soil; roots and worms probably contributed to the mixing process. As the city became less densely occupied space was turned over to gardens, market gardens and orchards. It took work to make this possible, and the dark earth shows that although the city was less densely occupied it was not left in ruin or decay.

Excavation has shown that on a minority of sites occupation continued unchanged throughout the second century, although on some of these sites changes were seen in the early third century (Rowsome 1987; Blair 1983). The upper Walbrook valley seems to have been least affected by the contraction of the late second century and the glass- and leather-working industries flourished into the early third (Fig. 36) (Maloney 1990). On a couple of sites elsewhere in London impressive new buildings may actually have been put up at this time; a stone building found beneath the White Tower had possibly been built by the end of the second century and a mosaic pavement found in Threadneedle Street may have been laid in the late second century (Butcher 1982; Jones 1988, 4). It is also possible that a masonry building with hypocaust and tessellated

FIG. 36 Foundations of timber workshops found in the upper Walbrook valley at Copthall Avenue (these buildings were set alongside the street shown in Fig. 32). Industry in this area seems to have been comparatively resilient during the later second-century contraction.

pavements recorded beneath Lombard Street had been built in the second century (Heathcote 1989, 51). The early third-century town contained several handsome new houses, although it seems unlikely that many of these had been built before the end of the second century.

Public building in the later second century

The forum basilica was badly damaged in a fire which has provisionally been dated to the mid second century, but the fire debris seems to have been cleared fairly promptly, the building restored and new floors laid. Although it can be argued that there were phases of comparative neglect there seems little doubt that the building remained in use throughout the later second and early third centuries (Brigham 1990). No phase of abandonment has been reported in interim reports on the excavations of the possible public building at 15–23 Southwark Street, and the same is true for most of the other sites of presumed public buildings. The Huggin Hill baths were, however, abandoned and demolished, possibly in the later part of the second century (Marsden 1976).

Revetments along the Walbrook may have been allowed to collapse from c. AD 155 and the water channels of Southwark seem to have suffered neglect in the period c. 150–70 (Merrifield 1962, 38–52; Wilmott forthcoming; Sheldon 1978, 36–7). In the upper Walbrook, however, watercourses were maintained until at least the middle of the third century (Blurton and Rhodes 1977, 20). The road system was little changed in this period; parts of streets found at Well Court, Milk Street and 24–25 Ironmonger Lane were kept in reasonable order even after adjacent building sites had been covered in dark earth (Perring and Roskams forthcoming). At least two of the streets laid out in the upper Walbrook valley c. AD 120 had, however, been abandoned by the end of the century (Maloney 1990; Shepherd 1987).

A new temple may have been built c. AD 170 (Fig. 37). Excavations on the east bank of the river Fleet, not far from Newgate, found the remains of a building which has tentatively been identified as a Romano-Celtic temple (Heathcote 1989, 52; Bayliss n.d.). Little of the building survived but a plan could be reconstructed on the basis of the wall-robbing trenches; a 16 m diameter octagonal central room, or *cella*, had been surrounded by an ambulatory 3.75 m wide. The roof had been tiled and some of the walls may have been painted in red, and part of a disturbed cement (*opus signinum*) floor was also found on the site.

This also seems to have been a popular period for votive deposits, and pits used in connection with fertility rituals are particularly evident. A timber-lined pit found in the eastern cemetery contained several mid second-century flagons, the remains of a heron, over 100 frogs and

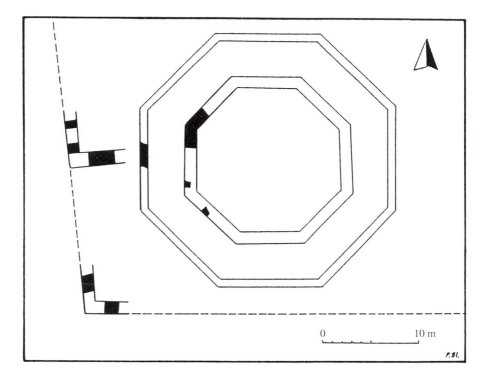

FIG. 37 The plan of an octagonal building supposed to be a Romano-Celtic temple found near the Old Bailey during salvage excavations in 1988 (after Bayliss).

various small mammals (Ellis 1985, 115−19). Another, at 1−7 St Thomas Street, Southwark, contained a wide variety of floral and faunal remains, including about ten dogs and much edible fruit and fish (Dennis 1978, 291−422). It was in use to the last quarter of the second century and also contained a few pieces of military equipment, including an intaglio with the military eagle and standards motif. This pit was on one of the few Southwark sites to have been occupied throughout the Roman period. Slightly further to the south, at Kings Head Yard, was a mid to late second-century building with tessellated and mortar floors (Bird and Graham 1978, site 10). Several pieces of military equipment have also been found in the area (Hammerson and Sheldon 1987) and it is possible that this may have been a public building or the suburban villa of someone with links to the army. It is perhaps also worth noting that a flagon bearing a scratched reference to a shrine of the Egyptian goddess Isis is supposed to have been found in Tooley Street, not far from this building complex (see also Heard 1989, 129−31). Sacred and ritual matters seem to have received increased attention in London during this period (Fig. 38).

FIG. 38 Pipe-clay fertility goddess figurines, manufactured in central Gaul and found with other mid to late second-century imports by the waterfront at New Fresh Wharf. Statuettes of this type, usually described as Venus figurines, were increasingly used as votive deposits in later second-century London.

Changes in the hinterland

Several of the roadside settlements around London also show signs of contraction in this period. There was a break of occupation from *c.* AD 150–70 until the middle of the third century, or later, on sites in Brentford, Ewell, Enfield and Staines (Parnum and Cotton 1983, 325; Pemberton 1973, 84–6; Ivens and Deal 1977, 59–65; Crouch and Shanks 1984, 3, 34). Although some of the evidence has been challenged (Smith 1987, 102) there is a remarkable degree of consistency between the results of different excavators working in different places; and until excavations start turning up the hitherto missing houses of the late second century it seems best to work on the basis that these roadside settlements suffered a contraction that was, if anything, even more severe than that seen in London.

The situation in the villas around London seems to have been rather different, although so little has been published that we are rather over-dependent on a study of the distribution of decorated flue tiles (Black 1987). The evidence suggests that the late second century and early third century saw more villas improved than abandoned. New building work was perhaps in progress at villas near Cobham, Walton on the Hill and Titsey in the period *c.* 150–80. Villas at Walton Heath and Beddington seem to have been built at a slightly later date, whilst there were phases of structural improvement at Farningham (Franks) and Darenth in the late second or early third century. Pottery from the villa at Ash also suggests a mid second to mid third-century occupation date. Only at Lullingstone might there have been a break in occupation, perhaps between *c.* 235 and 265 (Meates 1979; Reece 1987, 49), whilst at Ashtead there were no additions to the house between *c.* 150–80 and its desertion *c.* 260 (Black 1987, 35). There are also some farmstead sites in Surrey and Kent where late second- and early third-century occupation is as yet unproven (Sheldon 1975, 280).

Whilst it would be stretching the evidence to suggest that the late second century was a period of particular prosperity it does seem possible that there had been a modest increase in investment in villa building around London at this time. Resources which might earlier have gone into the building of a more fashionable town house were perhaps now being directed to a similar end in the countryside. The troubles of this period, whatever they were, were not of a nature seriously to shake long-term confidence in country property and villa society. It is probably no more than coincidence, but worth mention, that most of the evidence for building work dated to the period 150–80 has been noted on the sites furthest from the city.

The changing character of the economy of London

The later second century was arguably a turning point in the economic affairs of the province, and indeed of the empire as a whole, and London illustrates to extreme some of the changes of the period. In particular imported luxury goods began to be replaced by more locally produced wares, a trend especially evident from a study of the pottery. The production of Samian, and its use in Britain, slumped in the early second century and although there was a recovery during the middle part of the century there was a further slump towards its end (Marsh 1981). Eventually Samian came to be replaced on the British table by British fine wares; London made particular use of pottery from kilns in Oxfordshire and Surrey (Alice Holt). In the meanwhile table wares continued to be imported from Germany and Gaul but in more modest quantities.

There was also a marked decline in the amount of oil and wine coming into London. In Neronian levels amphorae make up about 40 per cent (by weight) of all pottery found, but by the middle of the second century this had fallen to 20 per cent and later Roman amphorae are comparatively rare (Tyers and Vince 1983, 303—4). It is also likely that fewer barrels, most of which were probably used in the wine trade, were imported after the middle of the second century (Wilmott 1982a, 1—78). It seems likely that wine was increasingly replaced by beer on the British table and olive oil may have given way to lard; oil lamps were little used in London after AD 170—200 (Frere 1987a, 285; Milne 1985, 118).

Imported fish sauce, *garum* or *hallec*, may also have come to be replaced by local products. About 20 per cent of the amphorae found in London had contained Spanish *garum*. One of these, which still contained a mix of mackerel heads, was recently found in Southwark on the Flavian Thames foreshore; the contents were advertised as 'L. Tettius Africanus' finest fish sauce from Antipolis' (Antibes) (Hassall and Tomlin 1984, 344). Excavations on the north bank have found that a Spanish amphora was re-used to contain a local brew of fish sauce in the late third or early fourth century. This was made of herring with some sprat, and a few bass, flatfish and sandeel; a catch which could only have come from waters to the north of the Bay of Biscay and was possibly from the Thames estuary (Milne 1985, 87).

The period also saw major changes to some of the larger industries in the region, in particular to those which might have been more closely linked with the provincial government and military supply. Pottery production at Brockley Hill reached its peak in the Flavian—Trajanic period but declined rapidly thereafter; there is no evidence for manufacture appreciably later than *c.* AD 160 (Castle 1972). New production centres at Mancetter-Hartshill and Colchester took over the supply of the northern market previously dependent on these kilns near London (Fulford 1977, 309). The kilns centred on the area of Highgate Wood also ceased production in the period *c.* AD 180 (Brown and Sheldon 1974, 230), and a pottery industry based in the Thames estuary which had produced fine wares from the Flavian period (Upchurch ware) seems to have faded away in the third century (Moynaghan 1984, 405—8). Salt production in Kent and Essex seems to have declined through the third century and the iron industry on the high Weald, which had expanded into the first half of the second century, was in decline in the mid third century (Cleere 1974). Although some of these changes, such as those on the Weald, need not have been particularly relevant to the situation in London, they combine to reinforce the impression of a regional economy less geared towards the needs of military supply and less well supplied by the goods which had previously been imported on military routes.

Although it is clear that the level and character of trade changed it is important to recognize that London continued to be a comparatively important port, and to note that trade remained at a surprisingly high level throughout the Roman period (Fulford 1978, 59–69). Later Roman London was still supplied with modest quantities of oil and wine, increasingly from sources in North Africa and the eastern Mediterranean rather than Italy and Spain; North African amphorae are first found in London *c.* AD 150 (Tyers 1984, 367–74). Dumps on the late second- to early third-century foreshore at New Fresh Wharf included plenty of imported material and commercial activity continued to dominate this waterfront area (Figs 38 and 42) (Rhodes 1986, 91). Finds from this site illustrate the changing pattern of trade through London. Coastal trade, especially along the east coast to York and the northern frontier, grew in importance throughout the second century (Green 1980, 77–8; Rhodes 1986, 94). London had turned to Yorkshire for its supplies of quern- and millstones; and even pieces of Yorkshire roofing slate and coal found their way on to this site. The English distribution of some north Gaulish fine wares of this date also shows an eastern bias which suggests transhipment through London, or other coastal ports, connecting with an east-coastal supply route (Richardson and Tyers 1984, 133–41). A series of discoveries demonstrates the existence of a busy trading community working between York and the Continent in the late second and early third centuries (Hassall 1978, 43); any direct trading links between York and the Rhine are likely to have been established at the expense of trade through London.

In addition to coastal trade later Roman London also saw a fair amount of river traffic; the pottery from Oxfordshire and Surrey is likely to have been moved down the river. It would therefore seem probable that the port of London retained a role, albeit a more limited one, in the economic affairs of the province and city.

The decline of road traffic, especially along Watling Street, seems to have been far more pronounced. This conclusion is suggested by the disappearance of London's suburbs, the decline of roadside settlements around London and the closure of the kilns between London and Verulamium. Watling Street ceased to be an efficient supply line once the troops were established in the north and traffic could be taken up the east coast. Not only were the supply routes reorganized, with the shift of emphasis from Watling Street to the east coast, but there was also a significant decline in the amount of traffic that would have been needed to support the army. The early second century had seen the creation of stable frontiers, such as Hadrian's Wall, and these created the secure conditions in which the army could begin to develop local sources of supply. Later troop reductions, and the rather modest and infrequent nature of later military campaigns in Britain, would have meant that the army was increasingly left to support itself from surrounding territories.

The context of change

London was not the only city to have seen contraction. Commerce seems to have been less important in several Romano-British towns in the third and fourth centuries; Verulamium certainly lost much of its early vigour and saw some suburban decline (Walthew 1983, 213−24; Frere 1983b; Stead and Rigby 1989, 11). Richborough also witnessed a serious mid to late second-century decline although it is not known how much this was offset by expansion at Dover (Cunliffe 1968, 243). Elsewhere in western Europe some of the most important and prosperous Roman towns saw a degree of contraction possibly equivalent to that witnessed at London; notably the cities of Lyon, Milan and Ostia (although in the case of Ostia the contraction could have been due to the transfer of port activities to neighbouring Portus). Amiens, a city closely linked with trade to Britain, may also have declined in the third century (Bayard and Massy 1983). These were all towns which, like London, had seen considerable benefit from the earlier high level of trade. In some of the richer parts of the empire larger villa estates may also have suffered economic difficulties at this period; a phenomenon evident in some estates of Tuscany and Picardy towards the end of the second century (Carandini and Ricci 1985; Agache 1975). In both areas the villas had perhaps depended for their exceptional wealth on an unusually high level of export. These were the towns and villas which owed most to empire and least to their surrounding territories; sites which had grown rich on the long-distance trade and traffic stimulated by imperial advance. The partial failure of these settlements suggests a weakening of empire. During the course of the following century this weakness was to become increasingly evident, and the empire found itself in grave economic, political and military difficulty.

There is a natural temptation, when faced with epic change, to seek explanation in epic events such as wars, famines and plagues. There had been fighting in the north of Britain on a number of occasions in the later second century, although nothing on a scale seriously to trouble the southern part of the province; and there may have been barbarian raids on the east coast (Frere 1987a, 135−49). There were also serious problems on other frontiers. In the 160s Germans had crossed the Danube frontier and reached into Italy itself, but these problems were resolved and the empire preserved. We know from Herodian that disaffected soldiers and peasants overran Gaul and Spain in the 180s. It is even possible that some of the British sites showing evidence of fire destruction in this period had been deliberately burnt, although there is no evidence that these fires were any different from the earlier 'natural' ones. Late second-century fires have left their trace in several Romano-British cities; in London, further to the fire in the forum, buildings were burnt in an

Antonine fire at Watling Court and perhaps later in the century at King
Street (Perring and Roskams forthcoming; Rowsome 1987). These were
generally unsettled times; but problems of brigandage and civil disorder
seem more a consequence of the uncertainties of the age than a cause of
them. Even if rioters and malcontents had succeeded in causing occasional
disruption cities are not wont to fall to such forces alone. In any case the
evidence of the villas around London suggests that any disorders of the
time had not seriously undermined local confidence.

A more likely *deus ex machina* for the disappearance of urban popu-
lations is plague. A plague is thought to have devastated western Europe
c. AD 165−90 (Gillam 1961) and might have been a contributory factor
in the depopulation of cities such as London. The decline in London
seems, however, to have started too early to have been set in motion by
this plague, and the failure of the city to repopulate at a later date would
also suggest that the changes were of a more profound nature.

An explanation

Roman imperial expansion had allowed the growth of a complex but
fragile economy, the weaknesses of which were revealed once the pace of
expansion slowed. Trade in the north-west had developed around the
needs of supply, the fruits of conquest, and the Romanizing tastes of
provincial élites. Once relatively stable frontiers had been established
under Hadrian and his successors, early in the second century, this trade
became increasingly difficult to sustain. With frontiers secure and troop
movement at a minimum the problems of military supply could be solved
without shunting goods across Europe. Private trade lost the subsidy
squeezed from military contracts and merchants found themselves faced
with escalating distribution costs at a time when developing economies in
newly Romanized areas were beginning to produce goods which had once
been imported. Italy had no specialized industrial techniques or productive systems to give it a competitive edge; provincial economies grew,
and did so at the expense of production in the imperial core.

The empire, tied to habits of lavish state expenditure rendered possible
by the profits of conquest, was also finding itself increasingly short of
bullion. These financial problems resulted in a progressive reduction
in the silver content of the coin issued in payment to troops and administrators. The reduced value of the coin, and consequent inflation, was to
have a deleterious effect on the drawing power of the military market and
brought sharply home the disadvantages of a ponderous transportation
system.

The consequences of this were not all bad. Many rural areas and
provincial industries were to benefit enormously; the villas of later

Roman Britain saw great prosperity, and some towns and villages close to frontier garrisons thrived. London, however, was hard hit by the changes. When conquest could no longer fuel growth the exceptional, and unsustainable, nature of some of the previous urban development became apparent. As trade returned to levels closer to those more 'natural' to the ancient world, the dominant role of the producer could be reaffirmed; towns and trade had never escaped the control of the landowning élite. In this situation some towns may have become increasingly inhospitable to commerce. High levels of expenditure were still required in order to maintain and glorify the city. Although much of the cost fell to city magistrates, several of whom found themselves in financial difficulty at this time (Garnsey 1974), there can be little doubt that urban rents, market dues and harbour customs would also have been squeezed for income. Later patterns of commerce were increasingly to avoid towns. Most larger-scale manufacturing centres in the later Roman period were rural, and the creation of rural Romano-British pottery industries from mid second century onwards, as in the Nene valley, may have been in response to the increasing burden of taxation on urban facilities (Fulford 1975, 130). In the later empire goods were perhaps more likely to be moved from one domainal estate to another, through tied agents, than pass through an urban market (Whittaker 1983).

Within a short space of time London lost much of its significance as a place of trade. Shopkeepers and craftsmen apparently disappeared from the town in droves in the period *c.* AD 150–200; a process which seems to have continued, on a reduced scale, in the early third century. The decline in the city population was presumably reason enough to close the city baths at Huggin Hill. City revenues were perhaps hard hit by the loss of rents and customs, and the programme of public building may have been suspended sometime shortly after AD 150. It seems probable that the urban élites remained, although many may have chosen this period to concentrate their attention on their villa estates. The city retained some significance as a port, as the local élite would still have required certain prestige goods, and it remained an administrative centre through which a modest amount of official traffic must have passed. It also continued to support a variety of industries; the leather- and glass-working industries do not seem to have been in decline much before the middle of the third century.

There is no reason to believe that the depopulation of London was accompanied by a phase of decay and dereliction; the organized demolition of redundant shops to make way for cultivated open spaces suggests the opposite. Perhaps landowners previously prepared to profit from shop rents were now arranging for their land to be farmed, a more reliable and more dignified source of profit. London was no longer a hub of commerce but had perhaps begun to become a place more fit for gentlemen.

6 The restoration of London (*c.* AD 200−250)

The town wall

After nearly half a century of comparative inactivity the city began work on the most ambitious and enduring of all its public projects, the town wall (Figs 39 and 52). This was built around the landward approaches to the settlement − the riverside may not have been walled until later − and enclosed an area of 125 ha. The wall has been studied on numerous occasions, and its remains still stand in several places; John Maloney has published an excellent review of the evidence (Maloney 1983), and the following observations derive from his work. The wall was built of Kentish ragstone, with tile courses at regular intervals up its height, and had probably been surmounted by a parapet walk and breastwork. It was 2.7 m thick at the base, where faced with a red sandstone plinth, 2.4 m

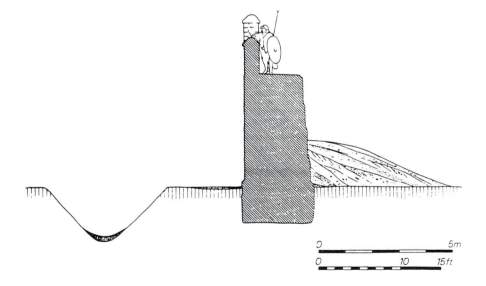

FIG. 39   A reconstructed section through the city wall and associated ditch at Duke's Place (by J. Maloney).

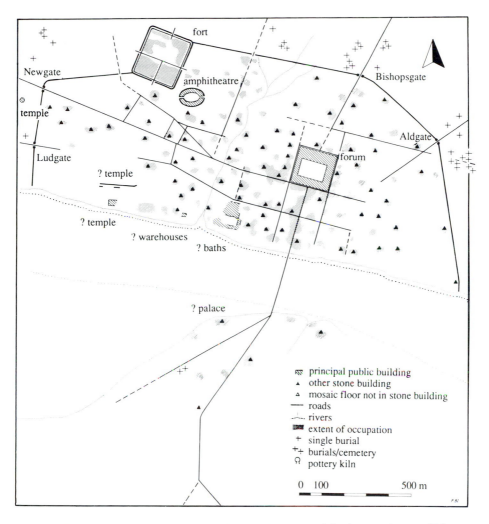

FIG. 40   Early third-century London, showing the extent of development in *c.* AD 230.

thick above, and is estimated to have stood to a total height of about
6.4 m. Culverts were built where the wall crossed streams; the largest of
these was an arch 1.07 m high and 0.99 m wide blocked by five iron bars.
The city ditch, set close to the wall, was V- or U-shaped in profile, 3.05 −
4.88 m wide and 1.17−2 m deep. Inside the wall was an earth rampart up
to *c.* 2 m high.

The wall took the most ambitious line possible, and its construction
may have represented a slight enlargement of the city from its previous
limits; the settlement had been reduced in density but not extent (Fig. 40).
In the south-eastern corner of the city the wall took in all of Tower Hill
when a slightly more westerly line might have been more practical. The
stone house found beneath the White Tower was perhaps of sufficient

importance to warrant the enclosure of this area (Butcher 1982). The north-west angle of the wall reused the corner of the Cripplegate fort and the fort's north and west walls were thickened to bring them into line with those of the city. There has been some dispute over the exact line of the wall in the western corner of the city (Grimes 1968); the wall has not yet been found in this area although recent excavations on the east side of Ludgate Broadway have found part of the later, flat-bottomed, city ditch (Frere 1984b; DUA 1987, 123).

Gates were built at principal points of entry into the city at Aldgate, Bishopsgate, Newgate and Ludgate; and those into the Cripplegate fort remained in use. Newgate had a double carriage, 10.5 m wide, which was apparently flanked by two square towers. This gate was not contemporary with the wall and could have been an earlier free-standing arch (Marsden 1980, 124) or an entirely later rebuild. Another gate entered the city at Aldersgate although its excavated remains show it to have been a later Roman construction, perhaps a replacement of an earlier postern. Posterns might also have been let through the wall at Aldermanbury, Tower Hill and Moorgate. Small towers on the inside of the wall have been found at the Tower of London, Tower Hill, Cooper's Row and Warwick Square. These seem too small to have been turrets, bastions or guardhouses, and perhaps housed stairways to a parapet walk (Whipp 1980, 47–67).

A worn coin of 183–84 was found in a deposit beneath the thickening of the external wall around the Cripplegate fort (Grimes 1968, 51) and it is difficult to believe that this coin could have been lost much before *c.* 190. The wall must be later than this. Finds from the turret excavated at Warwick Square suggest that the wall was in use early in the third century (Marsden 1970, 2–6). Fragments of moulds used to forge coins of Severus, Geta and Caracalla (dated to AD 201–10, 201–12 and 215), and coins, one a silver denarius of 213–17 in mint condition, had been lost or hidden inside this turret. The forger is most likely to have been at work in the decade or so after 215, although a slightly later date is possible, and it is probable that this collection of material had been brought into the turret before the middle of the century. It is also notable that excavations on the ramparts have yet to produce material evidently later than *c.* 200. The wall was most probably built sometime between AD 190 and 230.

In all the wall was about 3 km long and it has been estimated that some 30,000 m^3 (86,000 tonnes) of ragstone had been used in its construction. The quarries were in Kent, probably in the Maidstone area some 120 km from the city, and the stone would have been shipped to London along the Thames. The wreck of a barge carrying a ragstone cargo was found in the mouth of the Fleet river, by Blackfriars Bridge. This boat had probably sunk in the late second or early third century and may have been carrying stone to the wall. The capacity of this boat was such that it has been estimated that some 1,300 barge-loads would have been needed to finish the wall (Merrifield 1983, 164).

The building of the wall would have employed hundreds of people for several years, and would have provided a timely stimulus to the economy of the south-east at a time of apparent recession. It was the consequence of a considered decision made at the highest of levels; properly towns could only be walled with imperial licence, and required a considerable injection of resources after a period in which the city seems to have shied from such commitments. There must either have been some very pressing need, or a significant change in the circumstances of the city, for this wall to have been built. Before the reasons for its construction can be discussed in detail some of the other evidence for urban renewal *c.* AD 200 must first be considered.

Other public monuments and buildings

A large number of decorated stone blocks were discovered re-used in the foundations of a late third- or fourth-century addition to the south-west angle of the city wall; they have been the subject of a carefully considered study by Tom Blagg (1980, 125−93). Most had come from two monuments which were both civilian and religious in nature: a monumental arch and a screen of gods. Both were built of Lincolnshire limestone but in distinct styles. The excellent state of the stonework and the grouping of the pieces suggest that the original structures had been near by and were still standing late in the third century.

The arch, at least 8 m high, *c.* 7.5 m wide and *c.* 1.15 m deep, could have been part of a free-standing monument or a gateway through a precinct wall (Fig. 41). The sides of the arch were flanked by standing divinities; parts of Minerva and Hercules had survived. A frieze above the arch was partly filled by busts of gods, perhaps including the days of the week, and may also have contained an inscription, although this had not survived. The spandrels were filled by sea monsters and busts of the seasons. The character of the ornament has allowed Blagg to suggest a date not earlier than late Antonine or more probably in the third century, possibly Severan (i.e. *c.* 200). He also notes that a circumstantial case can be made for attributing the arch to a temple complex. The screen of gods was probably 6.2 m long and *c.* 0.55 m wide, and had been carved back and front with three pairs of niches in which figures were housed. Vulcan and Minerva, Diana and possibly Mercury, and Mars are recognizable. It is not clear if this screen had stood in an open area or inside a building and it can only be dated generally to the second or third century. Another carving found in the wall foundations portrayed four seated ladies, probably mother goddesses; an unusual piece since mother

FIG. 41 A reconstruction of the monumental arch, fragments of which were reused in a late extension of the city wall, showing it as a free-standing structure (by S. Gibson).

goddesses tend to come in threes.

The evidence presented by these finds adds some weight to the suggestion that there had been a group of religious and public buildings in the south-west quarter of the Roman city (see Chapter 3). It also indicates that there had been new building in this area *c.* AD 200. Indeed Merrifield has gone so far as to suggest that most of the public buildings in the south-west quarter might not have been built until the third century, and he tentatively suggests that the inspiration for this work came from the Severan imperial family during their stay in Britain in the early years of the third century (Merrifield 1980, 201; 1983, 170−2).

There was also large-scale alteration to the public building complex in Cannon Street in the late second or early third century (*see* page 32). Recent excavations beneath Cannon Street station, on the north side of Thames Street, show that a major masonry construction was built over the earlier waterfront (M. Burch and J. Hill, personal communication). Hundreds of piles have been retrieved from this site and hopefully there will soon be an accurate date for this building. The pool was filled sometime after the beginning of the second century and the large 'hall' to the north had been replaced by smaller rooms with hypocaust floors in an undated but possibly contemporary phase (Marsden 1975). This phase of rebuilding might also provide a context for many of the hypocausts and mosaics found elsewhere in the 'palace', and it is possible that parts of the site were now used as baths.

Large new timber quays were built on the north bank of the river in the early third century; quays, which added about 9 m to the depth of the waterfront, have been traced along its length for 45 m. This was the last comprehensive enlargement of the waterfront terrace which was now over 50 m wide. The front wall of this quay was made up of massive oak beams with tie-back braces secured by piles, although there was a more economical use of timber than in the earlier waterfronts (Fig. 42). The most thorough study of the third-century quay yet published, a detailed report on excavations at New Fresh Wharf (Miller *et al.* 1986), presents valuable but slightly contradictory information as to the date of its construction. The tree-ring dating indicates a date in the first half of the third century: certainly after AD 209, probably in the years 209−24, but possibly as late as 244 (Hillam and Morgan 1986, 78−84). Large quantities of pottery had been thrown inside the timber quay during its construction. This included two large groups of unused Samian: one of central Gaulish production of the period *c.* 170−80; the other from the Rheinzarben in Germany and dated *c.* 235−45 (Bird 1986) (Fig. 43). It is tentatively suggested that the earlier Samian had been old stock cleared from a shop or warehouse, or perhaps came from a nearby dump of damaged goods.

The pottery in the dumps associated with the construction of this quay shows that London was still receiving a wide range of imported table ware; indeed, the late second and early third centuries saw more beakers imported

FIG. 42   A view from inside the second-century timber quay at New Fresh Wharf showing tie-back braces secured by piles; the front of the quay is to the left.

than previously. Most of the imported wares found at New Fresh Wharf could have been shipped through the Rhine mouth. Some may have been imported to meet the demands of the wealthy urban population although it is also possible that some official supply lines were directed through London in this period.

The early third-century waterfront seems likely to have extended from Billingsgate in the east to Queenhithe in the west, a length of about 640 m. Work at 61 Queen Street uncovered part of a third-century building which

FIG. 43 Part of the collection of unused Samian found in the construction dumps associated with the third-century quays excavated at New Fresh Wharf.

might have been associated with the use of the waterfront (Burch 1987, 9–12; Merrifield 1965, site 125). It lay no more than 40 m to the west of the Walbrook and had been built with masonry walls and rendered brick piers, above a terrace wall. A large number of tiles stamped PP.BR.LON came from this site, and these might indicate the presence of a public building. This was perhaps a public warehouse and had apparently been demolished by the end of the third century.

The character and context of revival in London

It seems possible that the construction of the city wall was not an isolated event but one of a series of public works of the period *c*. 190–240. This, and the extent and quality of the wall itself, suggests that the wall was not a hurried response to crisis but a carefully planned monument, one of a series associated with the revival of a prestigious city. City walls served a variety of functions of which defence was not always the most vital. The importance of defined boundaries is illustrated by Hadrian's Wall. Built to divide the civilized world from the barbarian, a symbol to reassure those within and intimidate those without, it was also a most useful frontier. It was a barrier where small-scale crossings by unauthorized persons could be prevented, which channelled travellers to supervised entry places, and which allowed the control of goods in transit (Hanson 1989, 55–63). Cities too needed to demonstrate their power and authority, wished to control the movement of goods (especially where taxes may have been due), and preferred to control access. We have already noted that these were unsettled times and reports of brigandage in Gaul might have been quite enough to convince the élite of London of the advantage of a well-policed town wall. These élite were not, however, in a position to authorize such work and might in any case have preferred to stay on their country estates. The revival of London shows the clear hand of the state; the work required authorization and might, after bleak times for city finances, have required direct aid. The grant of permission to build walls might have been one of the best ways in which the provincial government could encourage local landowning élites back into civic affairs.

London was not the only town allowed to build defences in this period; earth ramparts were thrown up around several towns in Britain late in the second century or at the very beginning of the third. There are several rather different ideas as to exactly when and why these were built but they are likely to represent a positive reaction to a period of uncertainty (Frere 1984a; Jones 1987, 87–9). Walls were not the only protection that a city needed. To survive towns had to remain solvent — walls were useless if cities could not afford to man them — and to prosper cities needed the good fortune that only the gods could grant. These were not necessarily separate concerns; the construction of the Aurelian walls at Rome, towards the end of the third century, seems to have been part of a package of reforms in which religious and fiscal matters were given almost equal weight (Palmer 1980). London's wall, like that of Rome, is likely to have served as a customs frontier; and in this way could have earned its keep. Passage along the river is also most unlikely to have been free, and boats laden with imported goods would have incurred port duties. Inscriptions from neighbouring provinces suggest that the state was giving careful attention to the collection of such taxes in the late second and early third centuries (Keay 1988, 101; Drinkwater 1983, 84–5). The early to mid third-century extension of the waterfront would have created new land, quite possibly public land, in front of the old quayside. It is significant that such reclamation was seen necessary at a time when so much of London was lying open (Milne 1985, 143–4). Many of the old waterfront buildings in this area had perhaps become privately owned (Milne 1985, 133). The new quays might have allowed public authorities, or at least corporate organizations operating on their behalf, to regain control over the waterfront. There may, for reasons considered further below, have been a modest increase in state-sponsored commerce during the early years of the third century. These quays might have been designed to encourage this trade but also to ensure that the city could profit from warehouse rents and port dues.

The new city wall, the adornment of a religious precinct and the extension to the waterfront might be seen as interrelated projects designed to revitalize the city. These buildings both offered and witnessed a restoration of faith and finances – a promise of physical, financial and spiritual security.

The prime moving force for these changes to London seems likely to have been renewed imperial interest in the affairs of Britain. In AD 193, in the wake of the assassination of Emperor Commodus, Clodius Albinus the Governor of Britain became a claimant for the imperial throne. Albinus crossed to Gaul in 196 and was eventually defeated by Septimius Severus who also took considerable interest in Britain. Severus campaigned in Scotland from 208 until his death in York in 211, and according to Dio had intended to conquer the whole of Britain. This flurry of activity, with campaigns to organize and equip, elevated the province in imperial eyes and gave renewed importance to London, its principal city. Administrative reforms of the period, in which the province was divided into two, might also have stimulated a certain amount of activity in London. It has also been suggested that London had been elevated to the status of *colonia* by this time and that its early stone walls might reflect this status (Esmonde-Cleary 1987, 166). The period 190–235 saw much building work throughout the province and public buildings were built or restored in several Romano-British towns (Jarrett and Mann 1970).

Houses and élites

The early city had been crowded with the houses of an urban population busily engaged in making money; the third-century city was more sparsely occupied by a smaller population far busier spending money. Timber buildings had given way to clay-walled buildings and these were now replaced by stone structures, often large buildings with mosaic and hypocaust floors. Although the majority of the stone houses of Roman London have only been glimpsed in small areas (Fig. 44), often with little evidence for date, a small number of buildings have been more closely studied and dated. These suggest that the majority of London's masonry town houses were built in the early third century.

Houses of this period seem to have been found throughout most of the walled area. It is possible that sites close to the Thames and Walbrook were preferred, although these may merely be the areas where the Roman remains of this period have been better preserved. Perhaps the best known of these buildings is the winged building with a bath suite found near Billingsgate (Marsden 1980, 151–5). The north and east wings of this house have been investigated; each was bordered by a corridor with a red tessellated floor and several rooms in the east wing had hypocaust floors.

FIG. 44   Flues of the heated floor of an early third-century building found in Lothbury during the construction of a ventilation shaft for the Dockland Light Railway extension.

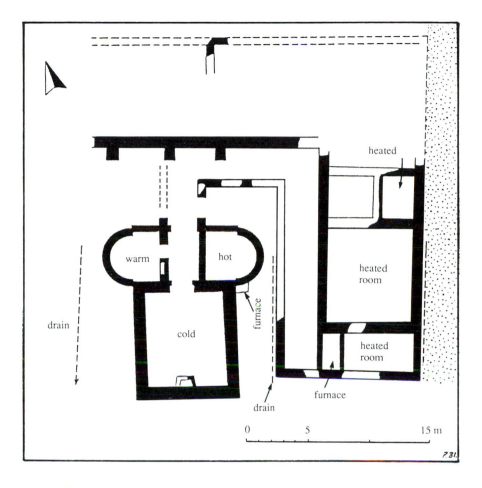

FIG. 45 Plan of a building and bath-house, probably built in the early third-century, found near Billingsgate (after Marsden).

The baths, set parallel to the east wing, were entered from a vestibule to either side of which were apsidal-ended heated rooms (Fig. 45). Beyond the vestibule was a square frigidarium which had a red mosaic floor and contained a small stone-lined water tank against one wall. This building has provisionally been dated to the early third century. Excavations not far to the east, at Harp Lane, revealed parts of two broadly contemporary stone buildings (Hobley and Schofield 1977, 56). Beth Richardson who has recently studied the pottery from these buildings concludes that they were no earlier than *c.* AD 180/200 and may have been built as late as *c.* AD 220/30 (Richardson n.d.).

Many of the most handsome buildings of Roman London were located in the Walbrook valley and several attractive mosaic pavements have been found in this area. Some of these have been tentatively dated to the early third century; several have stylistic similarities and it seems likely that they were the product of a school of mosaicists based in London at this time (Jones 1988, 10). Large buildings containing the works of this proposed school were found at Lothbury, Bucklersbury, beneath the Bank of England and at the corner of Leadenhall Street and Lime Street. Other early third-century mosaics have been noted at Pudding Lane, where Building 6 was extensively rebuilt at this time (Milne 1985, 140), and perhaps in the masonry house built over late second-century dark earth at 11 Ironmonger Lane, although this pavement could have been laid later in the century (Dawe and Oswald 1952; Shepherd 1987). The early third-century reclamation dumps at New Fresh Wharf contained a wide variety of building materials, including window glass, decorative stone wall veneers, tesserae, painted wall plaster and roofing slate (Rhodes 1986, 95). The roof tiles from this site included several new fabric types, and it is possible that the city was better supplied with quality building material at the beginning of the third century than at any other time.

In total there are records of at least forty-three masonry houses within the walled area which were probably occupied at some time between the late second and early fourth centuries; in most cases where dating evidence is available these were first occupied in the first half of the third century. If undated observations of stone buildings with tessellated floors are also taken into consideration there are about seventy buildings which might be attributed to this period. In those areas of the city which have been most intensely studied, as for instance between Cheapside and Gresham Street, Roman masonry houses are as thick on the ground as medieval churches. There were just over 100 parish churches in medieval London and it would not be unreasonable to suggest that there might have been as many as 100 masonry houses in the third-century town.

Despite the reduced density of occupation no parts of the walled town had been abandoned. Things were different beyond the walls and Southwark saw remarkably little rebuilding in this period. Excavations at 1–7 St Thomas Street found part of an early third-century stone building with at least one tessellated pavement (Dennis 1978, 291–422), and at the adjacent site of 4–26 St Thomas Street the northern end of a cellar in a large ragstone building on pile foundations has been noted (Frere 1983a, 313). There was also some evidence for building activity on the south bank of the Thames; the foundations of a second- or third-century building were found at Cotton's Wharf, some 260 m south-east of London Bridge, and a well dated to AD 231 has been excavated at Chamberlain's Wharf (Frere 1983a, 310). Fragments of a building possibly of this period have also been found at 10–18 Union Street (Heard 1989) but elsewhere in Southwark most of the sites abandoned in the mid to late second century seem to have remained open. There was no consistent revival here until later in the century.

Not all of the early third-century houses had stone walls; a few wooden houses remained, especially near the edges of town. Recent excavations at 76−80 Bishopsgate uncovered remains of an early third-century timber building, with a cement (*opus signinum*) floor in one room, which had been built after a brief phase in which the site may have been left vacant (DUA 1987, 46; Williams in preparation). The earliest buildings on a site at 43 London Wall were timber structures of *c.* 180−230 (Maloney 1990); and it has already been noted that some of the industrial activities in this upper Walbrook area had continued into the early third century.

The levelled site of the baths at Huggin Hill was occupied in the second to third centuries by timber and clay-walled buildings, one of which was set over stone foundations (Rowsome 1990). Peter Marsden reported the presence of stone-founded buildings, perhaps of a later period, in the earlier work on the site (Marsden 1976). In both areas hearths and industrial waste have been found and it seems that parts of the site were occupied by workshops engaged in metal- and glass-working.

It is perhaps significant that this rare instance of new industrial activity occurred on a site which had previously been occupied by a public building. Generally the commercial sector seems to have been in contraction at this time, but it is possible that different circumstances applied on public land (Mackreth 1987). The city might have needed commercial rents that private landowners would have scorned, or had perhaps intervened to ensure the maintenance of essential services; there is a considerable body of evidence to suggest that urban trade and industry had fallen increasingly under the control of the state in the later empire.

The lack of pressure on building space along the main streets of third-century London is especially striking. It is also notable that, in contrast with the earlier period, there was now no concentration of broken amphorae on the waterfront and around the forum (Tyers and Vince 1983, 303−4); the quayside had perhaps ceased to be a point where customers could come to buy a jug of wine or oil. Other Romano-British towns, as Verulamium, appear to have been transformed from crowded agglomerations of timber buildings into garden cities dotted with handsome town houses (Frere 1983b, 10−16). These places, like London, were left with only a handful of houses which were not obviously mansions or palaces. They owed little to the merchants and traders who may previously have dominated urban life. The loss of commercial vigour may even have encouraged landed classes to take a more active role in urban life. Suitably large urban plots could now be formed without any significant loss of rents, and there was no need to mix socially with uppity rich merchants.

The towns revived *c.* AD 200 were social and political creations; places where members of the élite classes had been persuaded to meet and compete in the guidance of community affairs, but which had little place for the lower social orders unless attached to the households of the rich. The city walls would have made it easier for the community to determine who could use the urban area. This process of more marked social division was evident in a number of other developments during the third century. Earlier ideas of community, built from the social structures of the city state, were to become increasingly irrelevant as the wealthy built barriers between themselves and their social inferiors. This had a consideration effect on the nature of urban society. Whereas in the earlier period wealth and good taste were expressed in the public sphere, with the consequent emphasis on public architecture, later Roman society placed greater importance on the individual. Private houses and palaces became more important than public buildings. Wealth came to be used to define the social divide rather than bridge it; this was not just evident in the buildings of the period but also in social custom and dress (MacMullen 1976, 72–3; Henig 1981, 140). It is appropriate that parts of gilded ladies' slippers with tooled designs, one worked to portray a head resting on a bolster, were also found in the excavations at New Fresh Wharf (MacConnoran 1986, 224–5).

The changing character of the later city finds illustration in London's most famous archaeological find: the temple of Mithras (Fig. 46). The sculptures and treasures uncovered during the excavation of this building, hard by the east bank of the Walbrook, confirm beyond reasonable doubt that it had been dedicated to the worship of the Persian god Mithras; its

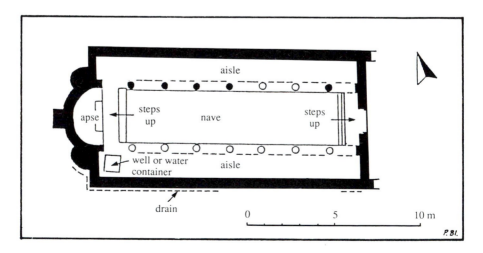

FIG. 46   Plan of the temple of Mithras in its earliest phase (after Grimes).

construction has been dated to the 240s on the basis of associated coins and pottery (Grimes 1968; Toynbee 1986). It was a small building, about 18 by 8 m, with a nave, aisles and apse, and it had been attached to a private house from which entry was gained. Columns divided the aisles from the nave, the floor of which was at a slightly lower level. The apse, where the altar would have been placed, was two steps above the nave floor; a timber-lined water container in the south-west corner of the building might have been used for ritual ablutions. Like many other houses of worship of this time it was a private place dedicated to the mysteries of a cultic sect; a place where the initiated few could engage in rituals which set them apart from the rest of society.

   The wealth and cultured background of the congregation were shown by the large number of fine religious sculptures which had later been buried in and around the temple (*see* Fig. 48). These included images of Mithras, Minerva, Serapis, Bacchus and Mercury along with several other sacred figures. Some of the better pieces were made of Carrara marble and had probably been manufactured in Italy during the second century. They would therefore have been at least 50 years old when the temple was built and had perhaps been moved from an earlier shrine (Toynbee 1986, 55−6). It has been suggested that the patron of this temple was an official who had been posted to Britain from elsewhere in the empire. Some of the pieces found in the London mithraeum hinted at Danubian influence (Merrifield 1983, 187).

7 The later Roman city (*c.* AD 250—350)

Temples and the riverside wall

Two inscribed altars of Lincolnshire limestone reused in late third- or fourth-century foundations in the south-west corner of the city provide further information on the temples of the later city (Hassall 1980, 195—8). According to translations proposed by Mark Hassall one of the altars reads 'Aquilinus the emperor's freedman and Mercator and Audax and Graecus restored this temple which had fallen down through old age for (or to) Jupiter best and greatest', although the dedication to Jupiter is not certain. The other announced that 'In honour of the divine (i.e. imperial) house, Marcus Martiannius Pulcher, deputy imperial propraetorian legate of two emperors ordered the temple of Isis ... which had fallen down through old age, to be restored' (Fig. 47). Pulcher, probably an acting governor of the province, is nowhere else recorded but the information given in the inscription, notably the reference to two emperors, suggests a date of 251—53 or 253—59 (Hassall 1980). These inscriptions might concern building work within the religious complex supposed to have occupied this part of the city. It is notable that a temple was in disrepair here by the middle of the third century; the programmes of rebuilding at the start of the century may have been followed by a period of comparative neglect. Whilst on the subject of temple repair it is perhaps also worth mentioning an inscription found in Budge Row which apparently records the restoration of a temple or shrine dedicated to the Mother Goddesses (RIB 2).

The other main building project of the mid third century was the construction of a riverside wall. It is probable that the city wall of *c.* AD 200 had not been taken along the waterfront and this omission seems to have been made good later in the third century. The existence of the Roman riverside wall, previously a matter of some uncertainty, was conclusively established by excavations at Baynard's Castle, in Upper Thames Street, where a tile-coursed stone wall about 2.2 m wide had been built over a chalk foundation raft set over timber piles (Hill *et al.* 1980, 57—64). This was the western end of the wall; the marshier ground by the confluence of

FIG. 47 An altar celebrating the restoration of a temple to Isis by the provincial governor Marcus Pulcher. The stone was later reused in the foundations of an extension to the town wall.

the Thames and Fleet was not walled off until later in the Roman period. Further parts of a riverside wall have been seen at New Fresh Wharf and in excavations at the Tower. Timber piles recovered from these sites consistently date its construction to AD 255–70. (Sheldon and Tyers 1983, 358; Hillam and Morgan 1986, 83–4).

There is a distinct possibility that the restoration of the temple of Isis, and perhaps of other temples in the area, happened at the same time as the building of the riverside wall. The dating evidence certainly points in this direction, and times that demanded new walls are more than likely to have required a little attention to the gods as well. The construction of the wall would also have brought masons and materials into town that could easily have been kept on for other useful building projects. The notables responsible for the temple restorations, a governor and an imperial freedman, are the very people most likely to have had a hand in the organization of the work on the city defences. It is slightly more likely that the wall would have taken precedence over the temple refurbishment and if this were the true order of events then the whole programme of works would have started between 255 and 259. The very fact that the city needed a new wall at this time, and that temples were in disrepair, suggests that there had been a certain degree of stagnation if not recession in the city in the previous decade or two. The rebuilding programme perhaps hints at state intervention to revive confidence in the city.

Whatever its purpose, the new riverside wall undoubtedly blocked the city from some of its quays, and there is evidence that some of these were in disuse by this period (Miller *et al.* 1986, 51−4). Access may still have been allowed at certain points; the Walbrook mouth would have been difficult to block and quays might have been found here throughout the Roman period (see below), but it is clear that the port was much reduced. It is now clear that this had happened before the wall was built and was not a consequence of its construction (T. Brigham, personal communication). Changes to the river itself may also have affected the port. At Billingsgate the partially demolished quay of the early third century had been cut by a river erosion channel. River-lain silts, which contained no material later than the mid third century, were then deposited over the eroded surface (Richardson 1984, 401). This pattern of third-century abandonment followed by erosion and then silting, in places up to 1 m thick, has been noted on several other waterfront sites (Frere 1988, 462; Miller *et al.* 1986, 30−2; Tatton-Brown 1974). It would seem that after a very brief period in which the tidal head had moved downstream of London, and the river began to cut a channel, the situation was reversed. During the period of erosion, when the tides could no longer sweep vessels up the Thames, London may have lost further ground as a port (Milne 1985, 85−6).

Britain in the period after 225 made few headlines − the province was becoming something of a backwater and there are few references to events here (Frere 1987a, 170−1). This implies a fairly settled state of affairs but cannot have been altogether good news for London which had always been the first to profit from imperial interest and expenditure. From the middle of the third century the real centre of regional power had perhaps shifted from London to northern Gaul, to Cologne and Trier (Salway 1981, 517). It is difficult to trace the impact of these years on the town itself; we know little of the subsequent histories of the buildings put up in the early third century. Some houses certainly survived this period

PACKING SLIP:

Amazon Marketplace Item: Roman London (Archaeology of London) [Hardcover] by Perring, Dominic
Listing ID: 0528R883687
SKU:
Quantity: 1

Purchased on: 25-Jun-2005
Shipped by: cherdoh@aol.com
Shipping address:

Ship to: Molly D. Shepard
Address Line 1: 210 W Rittenhouse Sq Apt 1008
Address Line 2:
City: Phila
State/Province/Region: PA
Zip/Postal Code: 19103-6850
Country: United States

Buyer Name: Molly D. Shepard

Saturday, June 25, 2005 America Online: Cherdoh

but we do not know how many were being well maintained and how many were in quiet decay. At 25−30 Lime Street buildings destroyed by fire sometime after AD 240 were replaced in the mid third century, the site being left open for only a brief period (Williams in preparation). Several building projects have been dated to the mid to late third century, especially in Southwark, although it is not at all certain that any of these were earlier than *c.* 270. It seems reasonable to conclude that the middle years of the third century were not as vital as those of the beginning of the century, but it is not as yet possible to determine whether the city was little changed or had seen some decline.

Soldiers and government

Officials and soldiers continued to play an active role in the affairs of the city during most of the third century. This is best documented by a number of inscriptions which have been found in London. The two altar inscriptions referring to government officials have already been mentioned. Further to these an inscription on one of the sculptures from the temple of Mithras informs us that 'Ulpius Silvanus, veteran of the 2nd Legion, paid his vow: he was initiated (or enrolled) at Orange' (RIB 3). Some of the military tombstones found in London are also likely to have been set up in the third century. Amongst these is that of Vivius Marcianus; the deceased was figured holding a centurion's staff in his right hand and a scroll in his left, and is likely to have been employed in clerical duties (RIB 17). Inscribed stone slabs found in the fill of a hypocaust stoke-hole of the palatial building at Winchester Palace listed personnel drawn from the cohorts of a legion, perhaps of *beneficiarii consularis* seconded to the provincial governor for civil administration duties. The names of the soldiers suggests a third-century date for the inscription (Hassall and Tomlin 1985, 317−22; Yule 1989, 35).

One of the most archaeologically evident military activities of the time seems to have been coin forgery. The forgers' debris found in the turret at Warwick Square has already been mentioned; a much larger collection of debris was recently found during the excavation of the city ditch at 85 London Wall (Heathcote 1989, 52). This material has been studied by Jenny Hall who was kind enough to supply the following details. About 500 coin moulds were recovered from the ditch, and others were seen in section but could not be removed. The forger was working from at least fifty-nine silver denarii (dated AD 194−253) and fourteen copper alloy coins, roughly one-tenth of annual pay at the time, and must have been active in the mid to late third century. The presence of moulds of worn copper alloy coins of the early second century is most odd since these coins would have been comparatively worthless; it implies that the money was produced to make good shortages in available coin rather than simply for profit. It has been estimated that up to 50 per cent of silver in circulation in the early third century was unofficial; it is possible that these forgeries were produced by the army at times when the stock of available silver was insufficient to provide enough official coin. The need to forge reflects the financial problems of the time.

In several parts of the empire the troubles of this age were not merely fiscal. For Britain, which seems to have weathered the period better than many other areas, the most worrying aspect of these troubles may have been the near total collapse of order in Gaul. Pirates and raiders also seem to have found freer reign in these years. Unsettled times tend to keep landowners close to their estates and the comparative lack of evidence for building activity in London may reflect such caution.

London shows some sign of renewed activity in the later third century. Excavations throughout the city, but curiously not in Southwark, have produced an exceptional number of unofficial coins, known as barbarous radiates, of the late third century (278−94). Many of these were scattered through the dark earth, and some had perhaps derived from coin hoards disturbed by later agricultural activity. Coin hoards were certainly frequent in London and Britain at this time (Marsden 1980, 164; Freer 1987a, 175). The predominance of unofficial issues in London remains to be explained, but is surely connected to the military presence in the city. Official issues of the late third century are comparatively rare and their shortage, with all that it implies about imperial neglect of the army, may have contributed to the dissatisfaction that prompted the British armies to back the British-based usurper Carausius. It is perhaps significant that Carausius once in power in Britain (from AD 286) established mints, including one at London, which produced a highly respectable coinage.

Carausius had been sent to Britain to clamp down on the piracy affecting its shores, and his very appointment may have derived from a greater imperial determination to tackle the problems of the period. A related product of this new strategy was seen in the construction or refurbishment of forts around the south-east coast, the forts of the Saxon shore. A mid or late third-century building found at Shadwell, about 1.2 km to the east of the City, may have been a watch-tower built at this time (Johnson 1975, 278−80). The structure, 8 m square, had foundations 2 m wide and chalk and mortar walls faced by knapped flint. Adjacent timber structures were perhaps barrack blocks. More than 300 coins were found on the site; most were of the period 260−95, with coins of Carausius and his successor Allectus predominating. This building may have been one of a series set to keep a watch on traffic up the Thames.

Another, and most important, discovery of this period was made in excavations at Peter's Hill; a full report on this site has been prepared by Tim Williams (forthcoming), and the following comments are closely

FIG. 48 General view of the site of the monumental building at Peter's Hill with the Thames in the background.

based on his work. The site, close to the presumed religious complex, was undeveloped until the very end of the third century, when the foundations for a monumental building were laid (Figs 25 and 48). The hillside was first terraced and a mass of timber piles driven into the London clay. A chalk raft, with a timber lattice, was set over these piles and supported massive masonry wall foundations. These were 8.5 m wide on the south side of the building and 3.75 m wide to the west. The north side of the building was formed by a narrow terrace wall. The foundations imply that the site had been occupied by a massive building which looked out on to the Thames. The piles had been felled in 293 and 294 (Hillam *et al.* 1984), and building work had started in 293 and proceeded westwards across the site in the following season. The astonishingly precise date which has been established for this building shows it to have been constructed at a fascinating moment in the history of Britain. Carausius had held on to power in Britain and some parts of Gaul until 293. In that year central government, now organized into a tetrarchy with two senior and two junior emperors, set to work to bring Britain back under control; Boulogne fell to Constantius Chlorus, the junior emperor (or Caesar) for the west. Carausius was soon after deposed and replaced by Allectus, who may previously have been his finance minister. Allectus, therefore, was responsible for completing the monumental building at Peter's Hill. This was not a military structure but it is not quite clear what kind of public building it might have been. The choice lies between seeing this as part of an extension to the temple complex — Allectus was certainly in need of a little divine help — or a palace building; work had started on the palace complex in Trier at around this time and Allectus may have felt it important not to be outdone in architectural propaganda. In either case a large building project might have served to stiffen confidence and keep troops busy whilst waiting to see what Rome would do. The wait was short; 296 saw the return of Rome and the annihilation of Allectus. Constantius is alleged to have arrived at London just in time to save the city from being sacked by the defeated army. The occasion is commemorated on a gold medallion found at Arras in France; the personification of London is shown kneeling outside the city gate and receiving the victorious Constantius as 'restorer of the eternal light'.

In the late third and early fourth centuries central government launched a series of far-reaching fiscal, administrative and military reforms in a bold attempt to restore the empire to its former prosperity. Earlier political structures based on the institutions of the city state had failed the empire in the economic and political traumas of the late second and third centuries and institutions of empire now filled the gap. Britain was now (AD 286−305) divided into four provinces grouped in a diocese under the authority of a *vicarius*. This reform may have restored some authority to London, which remained the main metropolis of Britain and would probably have been made the seat of the *vicarius*. London is also on record as having housed a central treasury (*thesaurus*) later in the fourth century. The office of *procurator* no longer existed but there was an official responsible for the supervision of imperial property, and another in charge of revenue collected in gold and silver and of mints and mines. The reforms resulted in an enlarged governmental bureaucracy and this is likely to have brought some wealth and work to London, in addition to the positive effect it would have had on the perceived status of the city. London might also have benefited from visits which were possibly made by the Emperor Constantine in 312 and 314 (Casey 1978, 180−93).

The local élite remained responsible for raising taxes, now generally collected in kind rather than cash, but civic office had for many become more of a burden than an honour; and those who could do so gained exemption from the duties of magistracy. By the end of the third century military officers and administrators had largely replaced traditional aristocracy at the head of the empire and were dominant in those cities which retained an administrative role. Provincial aristocracies were still made up of landowning families but these were increasingly able to direct their affairs from the countryside. The nature of public life had changed and this had an inevitable effect on the principal public buildings.

Public and religious life

The forum, arguably the most important public building of the earlier town, was levelled. The latest floors and surfaces uncovered in the forum at Leadenhall Court date to the late third century; these were sealed by thick silt deposits and layers of roof collapse. It seems likely that the building had been levelled *c.* AD 300, although it is possible that the apse was left standing (Brigham *et al.* 1987, 21; Brigham 1990). Similar changes happened to forums elsewhere in Britain (Frere 1987a, 247; Fulford 1985, 59–60).

By the end of the third century parts of the public building in the area of Cannon Street station were in a dilapidated condition, and a tile hearth and trampled floors were recorded in rooms on the lower terrace (Marsden 1975, 73–9); here too it seems unlikely that the public building had outlasted the third century. The Romano-Celtic temple outside Newgate also seems to have been abandoned at the beginning of the fourth century. The walls of this building were robbed *c.* 300–15 and a new masonry structure with at least nine rooms, and in later phases a hypocaust floor, was built over its site (Heathcote 1989, 52; Bayliss n.d.). The architectural fragments (Figs 41 and 46) that found their way into the foundations of the late third- or fourth-century extension of the riverside wall suggest that the public buildings of which they had been part were still standing towards the end of the third century but were redundant before the end of the Roman period (Hill *et al.* 1980). The palatial residence found at the Winchester Palace site on the south bank of the river was partly demolished in the late third or early fourth century, although at least some of the rooms of this building remained in use and coin evidence suggests that occupation continued into the second half of the fourth century (Yule 1989, 35). The massive public building built under Allectus at Peter's Hill had been partly robbed before timber-framed buildings were set over the site *c.* AD 340 or shortly thereafter (Williams forthcoming).

According to interim reports the walls of the amphitheatre were robbed of stone sometime around the middle of the fourth century and the building sealed by 1.5 m of dark earth (Heathcote 1989, 50). If this building had remained in use until robbed it had outlived most of the other public buildings of Roman London.

In those cases where timber structures were set over the remains of public buildings, as had previously occurred at Huggin Hill (page 103), it is possible that the city was attempting to find revenue from its public sites through commercial rents (see Mackreth 1987, 139). The changes recorded on these sites reflect the changed needs of urban society but do not witness its collapse; the later residents of the public building in the area of Cannon Street station could have been tenants rather than squatters (*contra* Marsden 1975, 78). It is notable that most elements of the street system were maintained well into the fourth century (as Grimes 1968, 134); although at 36−37 King Street the road leading from Bucklersbury had been covered by dark earth in the late third century, over which was part of a small fourth-century building (Rowsome 1987).

It seems possible that military and administrative changes of the period had resulted in renewed activity on the waterfront. Excavations at 14−16 Dowgate Hill found evidence for extensive late third- to early fourth-century reclamation of the Thames foreshore close to the mouth of the Walbrook at a time when earlier quays in the area were being deliberately dismantled (Frere 1987b, 462; M. Burch and J. Hill, personal

FIG. 49 The marble head of Mithras found buried inside the Mithraeum, showing also the decapitation fracture.

communication). There may also have been some new revetments of this period on the opposite bank of the Thames; reclamation has been noted in excavations at 38–42 Southwark Bridge Road (Grew 1981, 354). Much, if not all, of this activity might have been associated with the construction of waterfront defences and no port of this period is known.

The early fourth century also saw major alterations to the temple of Mithras (Grimes 1968; Toynbee 1986). The columns which had divided the nave from the aisle were removed, and most of the structure dismantled *c.* 310–20. A pit had been dug in the nave and several of the most important temple sculptures buried before the structure was rebuilt and new floors laid. Amongst the sculptures was a marble head of Mithras which had been deliberately broken by a sharp blow on the left side of the neck; this was the only piece which had obviously been deliberately damaged (Fig. 49). Further marble sculptures were found in the Walbrook near the temple site, there is little doubt that these were from the Mithraeum and could also have been deliberately buried at this time. The broken head of Mithras has been taken as evidence of a violent attack on the temple (Grimes 1986; Merrifield 1983, 211). Other Mithraea, on Britain's northern frontier and in Germany, were damaged in the later Roman period and in some cases Mithraic images had been destroyed (Richmond and Gillam 1951). Militant Christians have been held responsible, although the evidence against them is thin and circumstantial. The treatment of the sculptures only tells us that Mithras had been unseated from his temple, not how or by whom. Ancient images were always held to be potent and were treated cautiously; the soldier's effigy re-used in the foundations of the Camomile Street bastion had first been decapitated, perhaps a precaution to release any awkward spirits before building work could proceed (*see* Fig. 16). The most dominant ancient image in the temple by the Walbrook may have been sacrificed and laid to rest in order to prepare the house for new gods. Worship in the old style is most unlikely to have continued after these events, but the changes identified could signify no more than the change of ownership of the building; a new purchaser or heir may have been unwilling to continue patronizing the cult. Mithras was not necessarily suppressed. The old adherents may simply have changed allegiance, moved away or died off.

The refurbished building continued in use long enough for two more floors to be laid, a new timber south aisle built, and a pair of pedestals set on the floor in front of the apse. A small votive offering containing coins to 313–18 was found beneath timbers associated with the construction of the final stone altar base, and finds from in front of the apse included coins to 341–46 which date the latest use of the temple. Some sculptures and finds associated with the latest phases suggest that this may have continued as a place of pagan worship until the end. A marble group of Bacchus, with the inscription 'life to wandering men', was found over the latest floor and had presumably fallen there when the building was destroyed. A silver box and strainer and a silver bowl cut up into pieces had probably been hidden in a hollow space in the north wall of the temple. Other statues were found in the debris to the sides of the building; two marble figures found here had been hacked down to the torso; their limbs may have been removed for use as votive offerings (Merrifield 1977). It has been suggested that the later temple was Bacchic although the evidence is inconclusive (Henig 1984b, 113).

The fourth century saw the triumph of Christianity. Although church histories record that London was able to send Bishop Restitutus to the Council of Arles in 314, and may previously have been the site of the

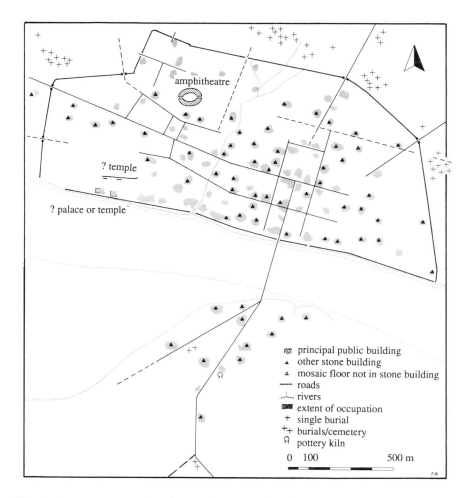

FIG. 50   Late Roman London, showing the extent of development in *c.* AD 300.

martyrdom of Bishop Augulus, we have little archaeological evidence for its Christian community. All that comes from the City is a scratched Christian chi—rho symbol on the base of a pewter bowl found at Copthall Court (Wheeler 1930, 25). There must have been places for organized worship within or just outside the walled area but these have yet to be identified.

Houses and settlement

Some houses were built inside the town walls during the later third to early fourth centuries (Fig. 50). New buildings were found built over the levelled remains of third-century houses on two sites in Lime Street: at Lloyd's building a stone house with heated rooms was built over a hoard of coins of 280 or later, perhaps a foundation deposit (Merrifield 1965, site 331; 1955, 113—34); and the piled foundations of a large apsidal-ended building found at 25—30 Lime Street are tentatively dated to this period (Williams in preparation). At 4—6 Copthall Avenue a site left open from the mid—late second century was also redeveloped in the period c. AD 250—300/50 (Maloney 1990). Building activity elsewhere is suggested by the fact that tile was still being imported into London from kilns up to 80 km from the town as late as the fourth century (Milne 1985, 105). It has also been noted that very few wells were dug in the city during the third century but that the early fourth saw something of a revival (Wilmott 1982a, 19).

Pottery wasters and iron smithing waste from a late third-century well in Southwark, at 107—115 Borough High Street, witness industrial activity in the later suburb (Yule 1982, 243—6) but in most areas shops and workshops which had survived into the early third century do not seem to have lasted into the later half of the century.

Most of the evidence for a late third-century 'revival' comes from outside the walls, in particular from the excavations in Southwark (Sheldon 1978, 39—40). The second-century buildings at Winchester Palace and 15—23 Southwark Street, and the early third-century complex in the area of 1—7 St Thomas Street were all rebuilt in the late third or early fourth century; an unworn coin of 270—73 was found beneath one of the new hypocaust floors added to the building at 1—7 St Thomas Street (Beard and Cowan 1988; Yule 1989, 35; Dennis 1978, 311). New masonry structures of the later third century were also found at the Courage Brewery site and possibly at the Tooley Street District Heating Scheme site; other buildings of this period are possibly indicated by building remains and debris found in association with late third- to early fourth-century wells (Yule 1982; Marsh 1978, 223; Ferretti and Graham 1978, 65—79; Dillon 1988; Graham 1988, 49). One of these wells, beneath

Southwark Cathedral, contained several important stone sculptures in its fourth-century fills (Hammerson 1978b; Henig 1978, 109—23). These included the figure of a male hunter deity, perhaps Atys; a funerary ash chest portraying a woman reclining on couch holding a bunch of grapes and a piece of fruit or cake; a tombstone; and a votive altar. These pieces perhaps came from the demolition of a family mausoleum.

From presently available evidence it can be argued that there may have been about a dozen large establishments in Southwark at the end of the third century. At least two of these (15—23 Southwark Street and Winchester Palace) seem likely to have been public buildings and were on sites occupied by stone structures in the second century; and most were on sites which have also produced finds indicative of a military presence. Finds from four of the sites (15—23 Southwark Street, the Courage Brewery site, 1—7 St Thomas Street and 175—211 Borough High Street) account for over 70 per cent of the military objects recognized in excavations in Southwark (Hammerson and Sheldon 1987); the inscription from the Winchester Palace site indicates that here too there may have been a military presence. Many of these finds had been lost long before the stone buildings were put up; it seems that most late stone buildings in Southwark were put up on sites which had previously seen a greater than average level of military activity. These sites include all of those with convincing evidence for continuity of occupation from the second century.

It is worth recalling that the suggested temple outside the city's west gate had also been replaced by a large masonry building in the early fourth century (Fig. 51). It is possible that the late third-century revival consisted of the construction of a dozen or so large houses on suburban sites which may previously have been public property. Might these houses have been built for senior bureaucrats brought to London by the reforms of the period?

After this flurry of spending on suburban villas little new seems to have been added to London's housing stock, but some properties were vacated and levelled towards the middle of the fourth century. Houses to the north of the forum, at Leadenhall Court (Brigham 1990) and Lloyd's building in Lime Street (Merrifield 1965, site 331), were destroyed by an early to mid fourth-century fire and not rebuilt; others near the waterfront, at Pudding Lane, were in decay by the mid fourth century (Milne 1985, 140—1). Whilst the city may have remained an important place for certain activities it is possible that fewer were drawn to maintain city property. The social and administrative role of the city did not demand a large resident population, more resources were lavished on the villas of this period and city life may have been held inferior to country life.

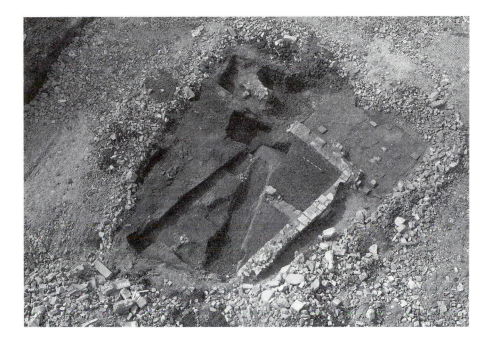

FIG. 51   The fragmentary remains of an early fourth-century building with heated rooms, perhaps part of suburban villa, set over the site of the octagonal 'temple' near the Old Bailey.

Villas and roadside settlements around the city

Villa society flourished in later Roman Britain. Many villa sites around London have produced pottery of this period and a few show signs of rebuilding. Several bath-blocks were built in the early fourth century (Black 1987, sites 27, 85 and 89), but generally the villas of this area were surprisingly modest for the period. There were even a few sites where occupation had perhaps ceased in the later third century (Black 1987, sites 84, 104 and 183). The principal villas remained those of the Darent valley and several of these prospered: Lullingstone, with its series of mid fourth-century mosaics, chief amongst them (Meates 1979, 73–4).

Several sites in this area seem to have built unusually large granaries in the period *c.* 300. Whereas most Romano–British granaries had a floor area of less than 70 m^2, three villas in the Darent valley (Lullingstone, Darenth and Farningham) had granaries with floor areas of over 275 m^2 (Black 1987, 126–9). These large new granaries reflect changes in the organization of the collection, storage or distribution of grain. Reforms of the third century had resulted in taxes being collected in kind with local magistrates responsible for their collection; later villa estates might have become centres for the collection and storage of such taxes. The south-east of Britain may also have been expected to provide some of its surplus in grain; it is recorded that a fleet of 600 ships was brought together to transport British grain to the lower Rhine in AD 359.

Most of the principal villas seem to have continued in occupation until the later part of the century; considerable numbers of coins of the later fourth century (post 367) indicate continued occupation at sites such as Springhead, Lullingstone and Darenth (Black 1987, 46). At Lullingstone the granary was converted to other uses *c.* 380 and a Christian house-church laid out. This villa, and possibly others in the area, is likely to have survived into the early years of the fifth century.

Roadside settlements around London witnessed a positive revival in the fourth century. Rebuilding has been noted at Enfield, Brentford and Staines, often on sites open since the end of the second century, and the period seems characterized by the introduction of some buildings with masonry walls and tile roofs (Ivens and Deal 1977, 64; Laws 1976, 182; Crouch and Shanks 1984, 3). At Old Ford a new, or largely new, roadside settlement grew up in the period after *c.* AD 270 and may have continued into the early years of the fifth century (Sheldon 1971, 42−7). The administrative reforms of the later third century may have served to stimulate a modest revival. Perhaps taxation in kind had promoted the movement of more goods, perhaps closer governmental control had put more officials on to the road. Whatever the reasons, it seems clear that the roadside settlements, like the suburbs, had been undergoing a not inconsiderable phase of renewal at a time when activity within the walls seems to have been fairly sluggish. It might even be that the period had seen something of an economic revival which had largely avoided the walled area.

One other possible cause of change in the countryside around later Roman London might have been the plantation of barbarian soldiers. The Emperor Probus settled defeated Vandals and Burgundians in the province in the 270s, and other land grants were to follow. These settlements would have been most easily organized on land already in imperial ownership and the Thames estuary might have been such an area. Important 'dark age' sites were later to be established in this area, as at Mucking, but it is not yet evident what relationship these sites may have had with any earlier barbarian settlement.

Cemeteries

The fourth-century population left little mark on the houses of London but filled the city's cemeteries. The main burial areas continued to be those beyond the gates at Aldgate, Bishopsgate and Newgate (Smithfield), and in Southwark; but locations were even less dependent on main roads than previously. The practice of cremation had gradually been abandoned and by the late third century all dead were inhumed.

The cemetery on the eastern side of the city has been the subject of a series of recent investigations (Ellis 1985, 115–20; Evans and Pierpoint 1986; Whytehead 1986; Frere 1986, 408–9; 1987b, 336; 1988, 464). Over 575 inhumations and 104 cremations have been recovered from this area, and an important study of the material is now in process. Several other sites have also recently been dug to the north of the city, as at Stothard Place and in the area of Finsbury Circus, and these complement the work on the eastern cemetery (DUA 1987, 193; Heathcote 1989). In Southwark late Roman graves were dug into the remains of late third- or early fourth-century buildings at 15–23 Southwark Street and at the Courage Brewery site, and were also cut into earlier timber buildings at Guy's Hospital (Beard and Cowan 1988; Dillon 1988, 3). Excavations to the west of the city have yet to add significantly to the material summarized in the report on excavations at St Bartholomew's Hospital (Bentley and Pritchard 1982).

Work in all areas suggests that the cemeteries were reasonably well ordered — at St Bartholomew's Hospital the graves seemed to have been arranged in clusters suggestive of family groups. A significant proportion of later burials were surrounded by calcium carbonate. One of those, at 15–23 Southwark Street, was of a girl aged about 12 wrapped in a shroud and laid on crushed chalk in a wooden coffin; she had been buried with pins, bracelets and an early to mid fourth-century cooking pot (Fig. 52). Some of these grave-goods may have been ritually broken before burial. Many other details have been recorded in London's Roman graves: orientation, presence of grave-goods, types of coffins and grave linings, etc.; and these may eventually allow the identification of specific burial rites. There is some speculation that the burials packed in chalk or plaster were Christian (Whytehead 1986, 55–8).

Some 60–70 per cent of the inhumed dead in the eastern cemetery were male (Waldron 1986, 115). There are therefore two particular problems to address: why are the cemeteries of London so crowded when the city seems so empty, and what had happened to the women? Both problems seem also to apply to other Romano-British towns (Esmonde-Cleary 1987, 198; Wells 1982; RCHM 1962).

Given the evidence for a very considerable reduction in the size of London's urban community in the second half of the second century, and

FIG. 52   The late Roman burial of a young girl found in excavations at 15–23 Southwark Street. The body had been packed in chalk, a practice which may have been favoured by Christian communities. Grave-goods, including bracelets and pins, can be seen to the right of the pelvis.

since all available evidence indicates that the fourth-century city was little busier than the third, it is possible that the size of the cemeteries is not a fair reflection of the size of the population. Changes in burial practice may distort the picture. The changing social constitution of the city might have had a significant effect on burial practice. The earlier city seems to have been dominated by its working population: businessmen, craftsmen, traders and labourers. Many of these may not have intended permanent residence in London, and might eventually have returned to their native communities when sufficiently rich or infirm; the cemeteries of early Roman London may not have received all of the city's dead. Cremation rites continued into the third century and might further distort the picture.

The later city might have been more important as a place of ceremony than as a place of residence; it is not impossible that city funerals became important social occasions, and men who had lived much of their lives in the countryside could have been brought to town for burial. Many of the dead were not, however, members of the idle rich; this is certainly the implication of the detailed study of the human bones from the cemetery at Cirencester (Wells 1982). Domestics and other serviles may also have been buried in urban cemeteries. These speculations are supported by sadly little evidence but might account for the improbably high proportion of men buried in the cemeteries. Not only were men more likely to have been honoured by a city funeral, but men also are likely to have dominated urban household staffs (Harris 1980, 117—40).

8 The final years
(*c.* AD 350−450+)

The later fourth century

The latest historical references to London as a Roman city are made in connection with two Roman expeditions to restore order to the province during the 360s. Problems in 360 were followed in 367 by a near complete breakdown of order following an organized barbarian incursion. London clearly remained the appropriate administrative centre for imperial recovery operations, and from these references we also know that the city had at some stage gained the honorific title of Augusta. The archaeological counterpart to these references, and the physical demonstration of Rome's continued commitment to the province and its urban order, were the city bastions. Bastions were added to the walls of several Romano-British cities during the middle years of the fourth century. In London D-shaped bastions were added to the eastern side of the city *c.* AD 351−75 and were set along the wall, from the Walbrook to the Tower, at roughly 50−55 m intervals (Fig. 53) (Maloney 1979; 1983; 108; Marsden 1980, 172). A badly truncated masonry structure was found attached to the outer face of the city wall in recent excavations at 85 London Wall and might have been part of the foundation of a bastion, the westernmost in the series (Heathcote 1989, 52). The bastions on the western side of the city were most probably medieval additions; for reasons of economy or indifference this part of the city wall was not altered in the fourth century. It is possible that some bastions may, however, have been added along the eastern end of the riverside wall (Maloney 1983). Similarities in construction suggest that alterations to the town gates might have been contemporary with the construction of the bastions, and a new flat-bottomed city ditch was certainly dug at this time. The extension of the western end of the riverside city wall found at Baynard's Castle may also have been built in these years (Hill *et al.* 1980; Sheldon and Tyers 1983), and the watch-tower at Shadwell was probably abandoned soon after AD 360 (Johnson 1975). It is also conceivable that Southwark had been provided with a defensive circuit which was reorganized at this date; a large east−west aligned ditch, in excess of 1.5 m deep and 5 m wide, was found in excavations at Tooley Street and contained fills dated to the second half of the fourth century (Graham 1988, 46). The defences of London had clearly been comprehensively redesigned during the middle years of the fourth century and there is every possibility that this was decided on in an attempt to restore confidence after the troubles of the 360s (Merrifield 1983, 235).

The years around the middle of the fourth century had seen several properties abandoned. The early third-century buildings at Harp Lane were still in use towards the end of the century but pottery from demolition dumps indicates that they were no longer standing in the mid to late fourth century (Richardson n.d.). Buildings at 76–80 Bishopsgate had also been demolished by the mid to late fourth century (DUA 1987, 46; Williams in preparation). The demolition and robbing of the house built over the temple outside Newgate seem likely, on the basis of the coin sequence from the site, to date to the mid fourth century; the area was subsequently covered by dark earth (Bayliss n.d.; Heathcote 1989, 52). In Southwark at least two late third-century houses were buried by dark earth which had been cut by late fourth-century graves (Beard and Cowan 1988; Dillon 1988). It has also been noted that the number of later fourth-century coins found in London is lower than would be predicted

FIG. 53 9 Crosswall. The city wall and the chalk foundation of a late Roman bastion built over the earlier V-shaped city ditch.

FIG. 54 Late fourth-century floors, including one of tile and concrete (*opus signinum*), in a converted warehouse at Peninsular House.

on the basis of the quantity of later third- to mid fourth-century coins (Vince 1990, 6), although the picture is partly distorted by the surprisingly high number of barbarous coins of the late third century.

Although the mid fourth century saw some contraction this may have been partly offset by a late fourth-century revival in the waterfront area (Milne 1985, 33). A house found at Pudding Lane (Building 6) was completely rebuilt with new heated rooms and a small bath; a coin of 367—75 was found in construction levels. Other buildings in this area were resurfaced in the same period (Fig. 54), and a portico was built to the side of Building 5. Some other houses seem to have continued in occupation throughout the later fourth century, notably near Billingsgate, at Peter's Hill, near Cannon Street station, and perhaps at the Tower (Butcher 1982).

There has been some suggestion that there was a movement from the countryside into the protection of the cities during the later fourth century (Detsicas 1983, 182; Reece 1980), but there is no real evidence for this having happened at London. Indeed all the evidence from London would suggest that this city was a rather frail and artificial place, and in times of trouble people preferred quietly to leave the city for the certainties of the countryside. City walls were built to reverse this tendency, with perceptible but brief success. We have no real idea of quite how small London had grown in these years. Whilst there may have been 100 or so houses in the early third-century city this number may well have been considerably reduced by the end of the fourth century; most third- to fourth-century houses seem to have been abandoned by *c.* 400.

The latest occupation of Roman London

The latest lump of monumental masonry known from Roman London was uncovered in excavations at the Tower (Parnell 1985). The north-east corner of a monumental wall, about 3.2 m thick, had been built just inside the line of the riverside wall. It was a neatly built affair and construction-phase dumps laid against the wall contained many fourth-century coins down to 388—402. This construction was perhaps part of a salient, with a narrow entrance to the west, built in the last decades of the fourth century. The latest Roman campaigns in Britain, under Stilicho, were of this period and an association has been suggested (Merrifield 1983, 226). Stamped silver ingots, of a late fourth- or early fifth-century type, have also been found at the Tower and there may have been a late Roman stronghold in the area (Painter 1981). Late military activity is also suggested by the discovery in London of a couple of bronze 'chip-carved' buckles, a type of ornament which appears to have been popular with the army in the late fourth or early fifth century (Hawkes and Dunning 1961, 62).

The campaigns of Stilicho were the last to be conducted by a Roman general in Britain. The next time that Britain faced problems the empire was no longer able to offer useful assistance; the communities of Britain determined to manage for themselves and, according to the historian Zosimus, expelled the last of the Roman officials. The final years of Roman London are difficult to trace. No Roman campaigns meant no new coin, shrinking trade meant few new imports, and Romano-British pottery industries were in terminal decline; there are therefore few finds which allow us to distinguish a fifth-century building from a late fourth-century one. Alan Vince has gone so far as to argue that occupation ceased fairly promptly *c.* 400, although he perhaps underestimates the problems presented by this scarcity of datable fifth-century material (Vince 1990).

The site which presents the best case for fifth-century occupation is the masonry building found near Billingsgate (*see* Fig. 44; Marsden 1985, 107). A hoard of coins down to 395 was scattered over the latest floors of the furnace room and corridor, and had perhaps fallen from a hiding place during the destruction of the building. The hoard had been brought together no earlier than the end of the fourth century, and the destruction of the building could have occurred some considerable time after the hoard had been assembled. A disc brooch of early Saxon type, perhaps manufactured in the early fifth century, was found over the demolition debris. This find does not date the demoliton of the building; it could have been lying about for some time before coming to rest in this particular context or been lost long after the building was levelled, but does suggest that there had been fifth-century occupation in the area.

There is also a fair case to be made for fifth-century occupation at Pudding Lane. The late fourth-century rebuilding on this site had been followed by further changes, including the construction of a possible sunken-floored building in the shell of one of the Roman buildings (Milne 1985, 33). Altogether this activity could have taken up several decades, not more than 100 years in the view of Milne, and it seems likely that some occupation had continued into the early fifth century. Fifth-century occupation is also thought possible at Peter's Hill (Williams 1982; Williams forthcoming).

The situation at London need not be so very different from that recorded at Verulamium (*contra* Vince 1990), although since the houses at Verulamium are much better preserved and have been more extensively studied the slight traces of fifth-century occupation are more readily recognized (Frere 1983b). In both cities a small number of houses, perhaps as many as a few dozen, might have remained in use for several decades after 400.

Cities remained the necessary symbols of authority for post-Roman communities which had yet to turn away from Rome as model. The new rulers of Britain, the magnates who had filled the political vacuum, still considered themselves Roman and attempted to maintain those Roman institutions which justified their power. The city would still have been perceived as the appropriate place for a seat of government, and urban palaces were maintained. Those public lands which had escaped earlier expropriation, and to which the new rulers were now heir, are likely to have been concentrated around the towns and might have provided another incentive for maintaining city establishments.

These post-Roman Romans, no longer held together by the cracked glue of provincial administration nor held in check by a Roman monopoly of force, were quickly to find themselves in disagreement. Rival religious and political factions fell out, and the peoples of Britain began to drift back to the divided state in which Rome had found them. Some earthworks built around London may stand monument to the growing divisions of this period. Grim's ditch, 4.2−6.9 m wide and 1.5−1.8 m deep, set on the south side of a large earth bank, stretches west from Brockley Hill to the river Pinn (Castle 1975, 274; Wheeler 1935). Excavations in Pear Wood, near Brockley Hill, found fourth-century material beneath the bank, although the south-western part of the earthwork, near Pinner, might have been thrown up in the pre-Roman Iron Age. It seems, at least in part, to have been a fifth- to sixth-century feature, and perhaps marked a boundary between the territories of sub-Roman communities centred on London and Verulamium. It followed a line which might plausibly have been the boundary between these communities throughout the Roman period (*see* Fig. 18). Another bank and ditch, on the east side of the Cray valley, may have been similarly placed between the communities of London and Canterbury (Wheeler 1935). This too was arranged to check traffic coming from London. Speculation as to the precise motive for the construction of these features seems fruitless as the evidence can support such very contrary arguments: London was a strong political centre with expansionistic ambitions and therefore the neighbouring cities were attempting to demonstrate economic and political autonomy; or order had collapsed in London and there was a tide of vagrants and refugees to be turned away.

A number of early Saxon settlements and cemeteries have been noted around fifth- and sixth-century London; finds at Mucking suggest that there had been a barbarian settlement here from the early fifth if not the late fourth century (Dunnett 1975, 140), and it has been suggested that some of these were settlements planted to defend the approach to London (Morris 1973). Some of the fifth-century cemeteries were closely associated with late Roman villa sites, as at Orpington, Beddington and Keston. Despite these settlements which ringed London the city has produced virtually no early Anglo-Saxon finds and it is difficult to believe that the site was still occupied by the end of the fifth century (Vince 1990, 46). London gained brief mention in the *Anglo-Saxon Chronicle*, written down in the late ninth century, as a place to which Britons could flee after defeat in Kent in the 450s, but need have been no more than a walled refuge; there is no convincing evidence for the presence of a permanent settlement here in the later part of the fifth century.

The end

Roman London failed twice over. The initial failure was essentially an economic one, the second a social one. Imperial expansion had powered an artificially buoyant economy in early London, and this could not be sustained once market forces were brought to bear: the commercial city did not really survive the second century. The new-model London, more closely in the image of a Classical city, may never have been such a great success; it seems suspiciously probable that Romano-British society remained essentially rural, with urban life a matter of form rather than habit. The role of the later city was largely social; Roman culture, which was urban culture, was the language of the empire's ruling classes. The political and social life of later Roman London may have come to involve no more than a handful of leading families and state officials. But Roman culture had no value if status, power and authority were no longer seen to derive from the Roman world; during the course of the fifth century the British commitment to Roman patterns of behaviour was undermined by the failure of Rome. Alternative cultural models, Christian, Celtic or Anglo-Saxon, came to seem more vigorous and better able to support some kind of social order. Of these only the church, the most direct heir to Rome, saw any role at all for the city; and the church was probably a significant force in the survival of fifth-century communities within the old Roman cities. But it was the barbarian values that were to dominate; and where Christianity survived it was as a Celtic and not Roman religion (Thomas 1981). Cities ceased to have a social role and were redundant.

Roman London failed, but its failure was not complete. Most of its streets were covered by dark earth in the fourth century, or shortly thereafter; and this seems to imply a positive attempt to convert a sterile cityscape into useful agricultural land. When new roads were laid out, several centuries later, some elements of the Roman street plan were strangely ghosted. Crooked Lane, Botolph Lane, Bucklersbury, and parts of Lombard Street and Eastcheap were laid over the lines of lost Roman roads; this was also true of Cheapside, Fenchurch Street, Bishopsgate and Fish Street Hill, although these might have been re-created from city gates and extra-mural street alignments. It has been suggested that the late Saxon streets were laid to follow earlier field boundaries (Horsman *et al.* 1988, 112); if the fields had been laid out in Roman times they might have preserved elements of the Roman town plan. It is difficult to believe that the city would ever have become a complete wilderness. If they had achieved nothing else the centuries of Roman occupation had created far too rich a soil to be wasted; London perhaps became a huge walled garden (see also Reece 1989).

The middle Saxon town that grew up from the sixth or seventh century had little relationship to the Roman city. It was a sprawl of timber houses and workshops; a trading and industrial settlement not dissimilar to those which had once developed around the first Roman settlement on the Cornhill (Vince 1990). This town was established some distance to the west of the old walled town, in the Aldwych area. Other mid-Saxon trading settlements were also established outside the shells of Roman towns; the defended areas were avoided. To our certain knowledge only the church was encouraged to establish itself within the city walls. A London bishopric was created in AD 604 and a cathedral precinct will have filled part of the walled area. It seems likely that towns were still considered as palatial and administrative enclaves, and as improper places for trade and industry; an idea of the city which may have owed as much to contemporary practice on the Continent as any record of Roman practice in Britain, but which was firmly rooted in late antique atttitudes to the city. Although it could not trace direct descent, the early medieval city of London was in several respects heir to the antique one.

References

AGACHE, R., 1975: 'La campagne à l'époque romaine dans les grandes plaines du Nord de la France', in Temporini, H. (ed.) *Aufstieg und Niedergang der Römischen Welt* 2(4), 658–713.

ALARCÃO, J. and ÉTIENNE, R., 1977: *Fouilles de Conimbriga, 1; L'Architecture*, Paris.

ARMITAGE, P., DAVIS, A., STRAKER, V. and WEST, B., 1983: 'Bugs, bones and botany', *Popular Archaeology* 4(9), 14–34.

ARMITAGE, P., WEST, B. and STEEDMAN, K., 1984: 'New evidence of black rat in Roman London', *The London Archaeologist* 4(14), 375–82.

BATEMAN, N., 1986: 'Bridgehead revisited', *The London Archaeologist* 5(9), 233–41.

BAYARD, D. and MASSY, J. L., 1983: *Amiens Romain: Samarobriva Ambianorum*, Revue Archéologique de Picardie, numéro spécial.

BAYLEY, J. and SHEPHERD, J., 1985: 'The glass-working waste', in Parnell 1985, 72–3.

BAYLISS, A., n.d.: 'Excavations and watching brief at 19–25 Old Bailey, EC4 (OBA 88)', Museum of London archive report.

BEARD, D. and COWAN, C., 1988: 'Excavations at 15–23 Southwark Street', *The London Archaeologist* 5(14), 375–81.

BENTLEY, D., 1984: 'A recently identified valley in the City', *The London Archaeologist* 5(1), 13–16.

BENTLEY, D., 1985: 'Roman London: a first century boundary', *The London Archaeologist* 5(5), 124–9.

BENTLEY. D., 1987: 'The Western Stream reconsidered: an enigma in the landscape', *The London Archaeologist* 5(12), 328–34.

BENTLEY, D. and PRITCHARD, F.A., 1982: 'The Roman cemetery at St Bartholomew's Hospital', *Trans. London and Middlesex Archaeological Society* 33, 134–72.

BIRD, J., 1985: 'Review of London, City of the Romans by R. Merrifield', *Britannia* 16, 353–4.

BIRD, J., 1986: 'Samian', in Miller *et al.* 1986, 139–85.

BIRD, J., CHAPMAN, H. and CLARK, J. (eds), 1978: *Collectanea Londiniensia, Studies in London Archaeology and History Presented to Ralph Merrifield*, London and Middlesex Archaeological Society Special Paper 2.

BIRD, J. and GRAHAM, A., 1978: 'Gazetteer of Roman sites in Southwark', in SLAEC 1978, 517–26.

BIRLEY, A. R., 1979: *The People of Roman Britain*, London.

BISHOP, M. C., 1983: 'The Camomile Street soldier reconsidered', *Trans. London and Middlesex Archaeological Society* 34, 31–48.

BLACK, E. W., 1981: 'The Roman villa at Darenth', *Arch. Cant.* 97, 159–83.

BLACK, E. W., 1987: *The Roman Villas of South East England*, British Archaeological Reports 171, Oxford.

BLAGG, T. F. C., 1980: 'The sculptured stones' in Hill *et al.* 1980, 125–93.

BLAIR, I., 1983: 'Foster Lane: the finding of the Foster Lane glass', *Popular Archaeology* 5(4), 23–7.

BLURTON, R. and RHODES, M., 1977: 'Excavations at Angel Court, Walbrook, 1974', *Trans. London and Middlesex Archaeological Society* 28, 14–100.

BODDINGTON, A., 1979: 'Excavations at 48–50 Cannon Street, City of London, 1975', *Trans. London and Middlesex Archaeological Society* 30, 1–38.

BODDINGTON, A. and MARSDEN, P., 1987: '160–162 Fenchurch Street, 1976', in Marsden 1987, 92–100.

BOWLER, D., 1983: 'Rangoon Street', *Popular Archaeology* 5(6), 13–18.

BRADLEY, R. and GORDON, K., 1988: 'Human skulls from the river Thames, their dating and significance', *Antiquity* 62(236), 503–9.

BRANIGAN, K., 1985: *The Catuvellauni*, Gloucester.

BRIGHAM, T., 1990: 'A reassessment of the second basilica in London, AD 100–400. Excavations at Leadenhall Court 1984–86.', *Britannia* 21, 53–97.

BRIGHAM, T., BROWN, G., MILNE, G. and WOOTTON, P., 1987: 'The Roman Civic Centre Project', *Archaeology Today* 8(9), 18–21.

BROWN, A. E. and SHELDON, H. L., 1974: 'Highgate Wood: the pottery and its production', *The London Archaeologist* 2(9), 222–31.

BURCH, M., 1987: 'Roman and medieval occupation in Queen Street', *Archaeology Today* 8(11), 9–12.

BUTCHER, S. A., 1982: 'Excavation of a Roman building on the east side of the White Tower 1956–7', in G. Parnell 'The excavation of the Roman city wall at the Tower of London and Tower Hill, 1954–76', *Trans. London and Middlesex Archaeological Society* 33, 85–133.

CARANDINI, A. and RICCI, A. (eds), 1985: *Settefinestre: una villa schiavistica nell' Etruria Romana: 1, La villa nel suo insieme*, Modena.

CASEY, J., 1978: 'Constantine the Great in Britain – the evidence of the coinage of the London mint, AD 312–314', in Bird *et al.* 1978, 180–93.

CASEY, J., 1985: 'The Roman housing market', in Grew and Hobley 1985, 43–8.

CASTLE, S. A., 1972: 'Excavations at Brockley Hill, Middlesex, Sulloniacae, 1970', *Trans. London and Middlesex Archaeological Society* 23(2), 148–59

CASTLE, S.A., 1975: 'Excavations in Pear Wood, Brockley Hill, Middlesex, 1948–1973', *Trans. London and Middlesex Archaeological Society* 26, 267–77.

CHAPMAN, H. and JOHNSON, T., 1973: 'Excavations at Aldgate and Bush Lane House in the City of London 1972', *Trans. London and Middlesex Archaeological Society* 24, 1–73.

CHITWOOD, P. and HILL, J., 1987: 'Excavations at St Albans House, Wood Street', *Archaeology Today* 8(11), 13–16.

CLEERE, H., 1974: 'The Roman iron industry in the Weald and its connections with the Classis Britannica', *Arch. Journ.* 131, 171–99.

COTTRILL, F., 1936: 'A bastion of the town wall of London, and the sepulchral monument of the procurator, Julius Classicianus', *Antiq. Journ.* 16, 1–7.

CROUCH, K. R. and SHANKS, S. A., 1984: *Excavations in Staines 1975–6. The Friends' Burial Ground Site*, London and Middlesex Archaeological Society and Surrey Archaeological Society Joint Publication 2.

CUNLIFFE, B. (ed.), 1968: *Fifth Report on Excavations of the Roman Fort at Richborough*, Research Report of the Society of Antiquaries 23, London.

CUNLIFEE, B., 1973: *The Regni*, London.

D'ARMS, J., 1981: *Commerce and Social Standing in Ancient Rome*, Cambridge, Mass.

D'ARMS, J. and KOPFF, E. (eds), 1980: *Roman Seaborne Commerce*, Memoirs of the American Academy at Rome 36, Rome.

DAVIES, B. and RICHARDSON, B., forthcoming: *A Dated Type Series of Roman Pottery from London, AD50–160*, The Archaeology of Roman London 5, CBA Research Report, London.

DAWE, D. and OSWALD, A., 1952: *11 Ironmonger Lane*, London.

DEAN, M., 1980: 'Excavations at Arcadia Buildings, Southwark', *The London Archaeologist* 3(14), 367–73.

DEAN, M., 1981: 'Evidence for more Roman burials in Southwark', *The London Archaeologist* 4(2), 52–3.

DEAN, M. and HAMMERSON, M., 1980: 'Three inhumation burials from Southwark', *The London Archaeologist* **4**(1), 17−22.

DENNIS, G., 1978: '1−7 St Thomas Street', in SLAEC 1978, 291−422.

DETSICAS, A., 1983: *The Cantiaci*, Gloucester.

DILKE, O. A. W., 1971: *The Roman Land Surveyors: An Introduction to the Agrimensores*, Newton Abbot.

DILLON, J., 1988: 'Excavations at Courage's, Park Street, Southwark', *Rescue News* **46**, 3.

DILLON, J., 1989: 'A Roman timber building from Southwark', *Britannia* **20**, 229−31.

DRINKWATER, J. F., 1975: 'Lugdunum: "Natural Capital" of Gaul?', *Britannia* **6**, 133−40.

DRINKWATER, J. F., 1983: *Roman Gaul*, London.

du PLAT TAYLOR, J. and CLEERE, H. (eds), 1978: *Roman Shipping and Trade: Britain and the Rhine Provinces*, CBA Research Report 24, London.

DUA 1987: *Museum of London: Department of Urban Archaeology Archive Catalogue* (J. A. Schofield ed.), London.

DUNNETT, R., 1975: *The Trinovantes*, London.

DUNNING, G. C., 1945: 'Two fires of Roman London', *Antiq. Journ.* **25**, 48−77.

ELLIS, R., 1985: 'Excavations at 9 St Clare Street', *The London Archaeologist* **5**(5), 115−20.

ESMONDE-CLEARY, S. A., 1987: *Extra-Mural Areas of Romano-British Towns*, British Archaeological Reports 169, Oxford.

EVANS, C. and JAMES, P., 1983: 'The Roman Cornhill', *Popular Archaeology* **5**(6), 19−26.

EVANS, G. and PIERPOINT, S., 1986: 'Divers coffins and the bones of men', *The London Archaeologist* **5**(8), 202−6.

FERRETTI, E. and GRAHAM, A. H., 1978: '201−211 Borough High Street', in SLAEC 1978, 53−176.

FINLEY, M. I., 1973: *The Ancient Economy*, London.

FRERE, S. S., 1983a: *Verulamium Excavations II*, Research Report of the Society of Antiquaries 41, London.

FRERE, S .S., 1983b: 'Roman Britain in 1982. I: Sites explored', *Britannia* **14**, 279−335.

FRERE, S. S., 1984a: 'British urban defences in earthwork', *Britannia* **15**, 63−74.

FRERE, S. S., 1984b: 'Roman Britain in 1983. I: Sites explored', *Britannia* **15**, 266−332.

FRERE, S. S., 1986: 'Roman Britain in 1985. I: Sites explored', *Britannia* **17**, 364−427.

FRERE, S. S., 1987a: *Britannia: A History of Roman Britain* (3rd edn), London.

FRERE, S. S., 1987b: 'Roman Britain in 1986. I: Sites explored', *Britannia* **18**, 301−59.

FRERE, S. S., 1988: 'Roman Britain in 1987. I: Sites explored', *Britannia* **19**, 416−84.

FRERE, S. S., 1989: 'Roman Britain in 1988. I: Sites explored', *Britannia* **20**, 258−326.

FUENTES, N., 1985: 'Of castles and elephants', *The London Archaeologist* **5**(4), 106−8.

FUENTES, N., 1986: 'Some entertainment in Londinium', *The London Archaeologist* **5**(6), 144−7.

FULFORD, M., 1975: *New Forest Roman Pottery*, British Archaeological Reports 17, Oxford.

FULFORD, M., 1977: 'The location of Romano-British pottery kilns: institutional trade and the market', in Dore, J. and Greene, K. (eds) *Roman Pottery Studies in Roman Britain and Beyond*, British Archaeological Reports Supp. Series 30, Oxford.

FULFORD, M., 1978: 'The interpretation of Britain's late Roman trade: the scope of medieval historical and archaeological analogy', in du Plat Taylor and Cleere 1978, 59−69.

FULFORD, M., 1985: 'Excavations on the sites of the amphitheatre and forum-basilica at Silchester, Hampshire: an interim report', *Antiq. Journ.* **65**, 39−81.

FULFORD, M., 1987: 'Economic interdependence among urban communities of the Roman Mediterranean', *World Archaeology* **19**(1), 58−75.

GARNSEY, P., 1974: 'Aspects of the decline of the urban aristocracy in the Empire', in Temporini, H. (ed.) *Aufstieg und Niedergang der Römischen Welt* **2**(1), 229−52.

GILLAM, J., 1961: 'The plague under Marcus Aurelius', *American Journ. of Philology* **82**(3), 222−51.

GIRARDON, S. and HEATHCOTE J., 1988: 'Excavation round-up, 1987, Part 2: London boroughs', *The London Archaeologist* **5**(15), 410−15.

GOODBURN, R., 1978: 'Roman Britain in 1977. I: Sites explored', *Britannia* **9**, 404−72.

GRAHAM, A. H., 1978: 'The bonded warehouse, Montague Close', in SLAEC 1978, 237−90.

GRAHAM, A. H., 1988: 'District heating scheme', in SLAEC 1988, 27−54.

GRAHAM, A. H. and HINTON P., 1988: 'The Roman roads in Southwark', in SLAEC 1988, 19−26.

GREEN, C. M., 1980: 'The Roman pottery', in Jones, D. M. *Excavations at Billingsgate Buildings 'Triangle', Lower Thames Street, 1974*, London and Middlesex Archaeological Society Special Paper 4, 39−79.

GREW, F. O., 1980: 'Roman Britain in 1979. I: Sites explored', *Britannia* **11**, 345−402.

GREW, F. O., 1981: 'Roman Britain in 1980. I: Sites explored', *Britannia* **12**, 314−68.

GREW, F. O. and HOBLEY, B. (eds), 1985: *Roman Urban Topography in Britain and the Western Empire*, CBA Research Report 59, London.

GRIMES, W. F., 1968: *The Excavation of Roman and Mediaeval London*, London.

GRIMES, W. F., 1986: 'The archaeological background', in Toynbee, J. M. C. *The Roman Art Treasures from the Temple of Mithras*, London and Middlesex Archaeological Society Special Paper 7, 1−3.

GUY, C., n.d.: 'Excavations at 60 Fenchurch Street (FSP 80)', Museum of London Archive Report.

HAMMER, F., 1985: 'Early Roman buildings in Fenchurch Street', *Popular Archaeology* **6**(12), 7−13.

HAMMER, F., 1987: 'A Roman basilica hall and associated buildings at Fenchurch Street', *Archaeology Today* **8**(9), 6−12.

HAMMERSON, M., 1978a: 'Coins', in SLAEC 1978, 587−600.

HAMMERSON, M., 1978b: 'Excavations under Southwark Cathedral', *The London Archaeologist* **3**(8), 206−12.

HAMMERSON, M., 1988: 'Roman coins from Southwark', in SLAEC 1988, 417−26.

HAMMERSON, M. and SHELDON, H., 1987: 'Evidence for the Roman army in Southwark', in Dawson, M. (ed.) *Roman Military Equipment, The Accoutrements of War*, British Archaeological Reports Suppl. Series 336, Oxford, 167−73.

HANSON, W. S., 1989: 'The nature and function of Roman frontiers', in Barrett, J. C., Fitzpatrick, A. P. and Macinnes, L. (eds) *Barbarians and Romans in North-West Europe*, British Archaeological Reports Suppl. Series 471, Oxford, 55−63.

HARRIS, W. V., 1980: 'Towards a study of the Roman slave trade', in D'Arms and Kopff 1980, 117−40.

HASELGROVE, C., 1988: 'The archaeology of British potin coinage', *Arch. Journ.* **145**, 99−122.

HASSALL, M. W. C., 1973: 'Roman Soldiers in Roman London', in Strong, D. E. (ed.) *Archaeological Theory and Practice*, London, 231−7.

HASSALL, M. W. C., 1978: 'Britain and the Rhine provinces: epigraphic evidence for Roman trade', in du Plat Taylor and Cleere 1978, 41−8.

HASSALL, M. W. C., 1980: 'The inscribed altars', in Hill *et al.* 1980, 195−7.

HASSALL, M. W. C. and TOMLIN, R. S. O., 1984: 'Roman Britain in 1983: II. Inscriptions', *Britannia* 15, 333–56.

HASSALL, M. W. C. and TOMLIN, R. S. O., 1985: 'Roman Britain in 1984: II. Inscriptions', *Britannia*, 16, 317–32.

HASSALL, M. W. C. and TOMLIN, R. S. O., 1987: 'Roman Britain in 1986: II. Inscriptions', *Britannia* 18, 360–77.

HAVERFIELD, F., 1911: 'Roman London', *Journal of Roman Studies* 1, 141–72.

HAWKES, S. C. and DUNNING G. C., 1961: 'Soldiers and settlers in Britain, fourth to fifth century: with a catalogue of animal-ornamented buckles and related belt-fittings', *Medieval Archaeology* 5, 1–70.

HEARD, K., 1989: 'Excavations at 10–18 Union Street, Southwark', *The London Archaeologist* 6(5), 126–31.

HEATHCOTE, J., 1989: 'Excavation round-up 1988, Part 1: City of London', *The London Archaeologist* 6(2); 46–53.

HENIG, M., 1978: 'Some reflections of Greek sculpture and painting in Roman art from London', in Bird *et al.* 1978, 109–23.

HENIG, M., 1981: 'Continuity and change in the design of Roman jewellery', in King, A. C. and Henig, M. (eds), *The Roman West in the Third Century* British Archaeological Reports Suppl. Series 109, 127–43.

HENIG, M., 1984a: *Religion in Roman Britain*, London.

HENIG, M., 1984b: 'A cache of Roman intaglios from Eastcheap, City of London', *Trans. London and Middlesex Archaeological Society* 35, 11–15.

HILL, C., MILLETT, M. and BLAGG, T., 1980: *The Roman Riverside Wall and Monumental Arch in London: Excavations at Baynard's Castle, Upper Thames Street*, London 1974–76, London and Middlesex Archaeological Society Special Paper 3.

HILLAM, J. and MORGAN, R. A., 1986: 'Tree-ring analysis of the Roman timbers', in Miller *et al.* 1986, 75–86.

HILLAM, J., MORGAN, R. A. and TYERS, I., 1984: 'Dendrochronology and Roman London', *Trans. London and Middlesex Archaeological Society* 35, 1–4.

HOBLEY, B. and SCHOFIELD, J. A., 1977: 'Excavations in the City of London, first interim report 1974–5', *Antiq. Journ.* 57(1), 31–66.

HOPKINS, K., 1978: 'Economic growth and towns in Classical Antiquity', in Abrams, P. and Wrigley, E. A. (eds) *Towns and Societies*, 35–79.

HORSEMAN, V., MILNE C. and MILNE G., 1988: *Aspects of Saxo-Norman London*, London and Middlesex Archaeological Society Special Paper 11.

HOUSTON, G. W., 1988: 'Ports in perspective: some comparative materials on Roman merchant ships and ports', *American Journal of Archaeology* 92, 553–64.

HUGGINS, R., 1986: Letter to *The London Archaeologist* 5(7), 195.

HUMPHREY, J. H., 1986: *Roman Circuses*, London.

IVENS, J. and DEAL, G., 1977: 'Finds and excavations in Roman Enfield', *The London Archaeologist* 3(3), 59–65.

JARRETT, M. G. and MANN, J. C., 1970: 'Britain from Agricola to Gallienus', *Bonner Jahrbuch* 170, 178–210.

JASHEMSKI, W., 1979: *The Gardens of Pompeii*, New Rochelle (N.Y.).

JOHNSON, T., 1975: 'A Roman signal station at Shadwell, E.1.', *Trans. London and Middlesex Archaeological Society* 26, 278–80.

JONES, C. E. E., 1983: 'A review of Roman lead-alloy material recovered from the Walbrook valley in the city of London', *Trans. London and Middlesex Archaeological Society* 34, 49–59.

JONES, C., 1988: *Roman Mosaics*, Museum of London: the London Connection 6, London.

JONES, M. J., 1987: 'Roman defences', in Schofield and Leech 1987, 81–92.

KEAY, S. J., 1988: *Roman Spain*, London.

KENT, J., 1978: 'The London area in the late iron age: an interpretation of the earliest coins', in Bird *et al.* 1978, 53–8.

KEYS, D., 1988: 'Greetings from AD 110', *Illustrated London News* 276, Dec., 54.

LAWS, A., 1976: 'Excavations at Northumberland Wharf, Brentford', *Trans. London and Middlesex Archaeological Society* 27, 179–205.

LEES, D., WOODGER, A. and ORTON C., 1989; 'Excavations in the Walbrook valley', *The London Archaeologist* 6(5), 115–19.

LING, R., 1989: 'Lullingstone and the study of wall painting in Britain', *Journal of Roman Archaeology* 2, 378–84.

MCCANN, B. and ORTON, C., 1989: 'The Fleet valley project', *The London Archaeologist* 6(4), 102–7.

MACCONNORAN, P., 'Footwear', in Miller *et al.*, 218–26.

MACKRETH, D. F., 1987: 'Roman public buildings', in Schofield and Leech 1987, 133–46.

MACMULLEN, R., 1976: *Roman Governments' Response to Crisis AD 235–337*, New Haven, London.

MCWHIRR, A., 1986: *Houses in Roman Cirencester*, Cirencester Excavations 3, Cirencester.

MALONEY, C., with de Moulins, D., 1990: *The Upper Walbrook Valley*, The Archaeology of Roman London 1, CBA Research Report 69, London.

MALONEY, J., 1979: 'The excavations at Duke's Place: the Roman defences', *The London Archaeologist* 3(11), 292–7.

MALONEY, J., 1983: 'Recent work on London's defences', in Maloney, J. and Hobley, B. (eds) *Roman Urban Defences in the West*, CBA Research Report 51, London, 96–117.

MARGARY, I. D., 1967: *Roman Roads in Britain* (2nd edn), London.

MARSDEN, P., 1967: 'The riverside defensive wall of Roman London', *Trans. London and Middlesex Archaeological Society* 21(3), 149–56.

MARSDEN, P., 1968: 'Archaeological finds in the City of London, 1965–6', *Trans. London and Middlesex Archaeological Society* 22(1), 1–17.

MARSDEN, P., 1969: 'The Roman pottery industry of London', *Trans. London and Middlesex Archaeological Society* 22(2), 39–44.

MARSDEN, P., 1970: 'Archaeological finds in the City of London, 1966–9', *Trans. London and Middlesex Archaeological Society* 22(3), 1–9.

MARSDEN, P., 1971: 'Report on recent excavations in Southwark: Part II', *Trans. London Middlesex Archaeological Society* 23(1), 19–41.

MARSDEN, P., 1975: 'The excavation of a Roman palace site in London, 1961–1972', *Trans. London and Middlesex Archaeological Society* 26, 1–102.

MARSDEN, P., 1976: 'Two Roman public baths in London', *Trans. London and Middlesex Archaeological Society* 27, 2–70.

MARSDEN, P., 1978: 'The excavation of a Roman palace site in London: additional details', *Trans. London and Middlesex Archaeological Society* 29, 99–103.

MARSDEN, P., 1980: *Roman London*, London.

MARSDEN, P., 1985: 'London in the 3rd and 4th centuries', in Grew and Hobley 1985, 99–108.

MARSDEN, P., 1987: *The Roman Forum Site in London: Discoveries before 1985*, HMSO, London.

MARSH, G., 1978: '8 Union Street', in SLAEC 1978, 221–32.

MARSH, G., 1981: 'London's Samian supply and its relationship to the development of the Gallic Samian industry', in Anderson, A. C. and A. S. (eds) *Roman Pottery Research in Britain and North-West Europe. Papers presented to Graham Webster*, British Archaeological Reports Suppl. Series 13, Oxford, 173–238.

MARSH, G. and TYERS, P., 1976: 'Roman pottery from the City of London', *Trans. London and Middlesex Archaeological Society* 27, 228–44.

MARSH, G. and TYERS, P., 1978: 'The Roman pottery from Southwark', in SLAEC 1978, 533–86.

MARSH, G. and WEST, B., 1981: 'Skullduggery in Roman London', *Trans. London and Middlesex Archaeological Society* 32, 86–102.

MEATES, G. W., 1979: *The Lullingstone Roman Villa, 1: The Site*, Kent Archaeological Society Monograph 1, Maidstone.

MEIGGS, R., 1973: *Roman Ostia* (2nd edn), Oxford.

MERRIFIELD, R., 1955: 'The Lime Street hoard of barbarous radiates', *Numismatic Chronicle* 6(15), 113–34.

MERRIFIELD, R., 1962: 'Coins from the bed of the Walbrook, and their significance', *Antiq. Journ.* 62, 38–52.

MERRIFIELD, R., 1965: *The Roman City of London*. London.

MERRIFIELD, R., 1977: 'Art and religion in Roman London – an inquest on the sculptures of Londinium', in Munby, J. and M. Henig, (eds) *Roman Life and Art in Britain*, British Archaeological Reports 41, Oxford, 389–90.

MERRIFIELD, R., 1980: 'The contribution to our knowledge of Roman London', in Hill *et al.* 1980, 200–5.

MERRIFIELD, R., 1983: *London, City of the Romans*, London.

MERRIMAN, N., 1987: 'A prehistory for Central London', *The London Archaeologist* 5(12), 318–26.

MIDDLETON, P., 1979: 'Army supply in Roman Gaul: an hypothesis for Roman Britain', in Burnham, B. C. and Johnson, H. B. (eds) *Invasion and Response: The Case of Roman Britain*, British Archaeological Reports 73, Oxford, 81–97.

MILLER, L., SCHFIELD, J. and RHODES, M., 1986: *The Roman Quay at St Magnus House, London*, London and Middlesex Archaeological Society, Special Paper 8.

MILLETT, M., 1987: 'Boudicca, the first Colchester potters' shop, and the dating of Neronian Samian', *Britannia* 18, 93–123.

MILNE, G. (ed.) 1985: *The Port of Roman London*, London.

MILNE, G., BATEMAN, N. and MILNE, C., 1984: 'Bank deposits with interest', *The London Archaeologoist* 4(15). 395–400.

MORRIS, J., 1973: *The Age of Arthur*, London.

MORRIS, J., 1975: 'London's decline AD 150–250', *The London Archaeologist* 2(13), 343–4.

MORRIS, J., 1982: *Londinium, London in the Roman Empire*, London.

MOYNAGHAN, J., 1984: 'Upchurch fine ware', *The London Archaeologist* 4(15), 405–8.

NIBLETT, R., 1985: *Sheepen: An Early Roman Industrial Site at Camulodunum*, CBA Research Report 57, London.

NORMAN, P. and READER, F. W., 1912: 'Further discoveries relating to Roman London, 1906–12', *Archaeologia* 63, 257–344.

NORTON, J., 1982: 'Ironmonger Lane', *The London Archaeologist* 4.7, 171–5.

PAINTER, K. S., 1963: 'A Roman tombstone from Holborn', *Antiq. Journ.* 43, 123–8.

PAINTER, K. S., 1981: 'A Roman silver ingot', *Department of Greek and Roman Antiquities, Acquisitions 1976*, B.M. Occasional Paper 35.

PALMER, R. E. A., 1980: 'Customs on market goods imported into the city of Rome', in D'Arms and Kopff 1980, 217–33.

PARNELL, G., 1985: 'The Roman and medieval defences and the later development of the Inmost Ward, Tower of London: excavations 1955–77', *Trans. London and Middlesex Archaeological Society* 36, 1–75.

PARNUM, A. and COTTON, J., 1983: 'Recent work in Brentford: excavations and observations 1974–82', *The London Archaeologist* 4(12), 318–25.

PEMBERTON, F., 1973: 'A Romano-British settlement on Stane Street, Ewell, Surrey', *Surrey Arch. Coll's.* **69** 1–26.

PERRING, D. and ROSKAMS, S. P. with Allen P., forthcoming: *The Early Development of Roman London to the West of the Walbrook*, The Archaeology of Roman London 2, CBA Research Report 70, London.

PHILP, B. J., 1977: 'The forum of Roman London', *Britannia* **8**, 1–64.

POLLARD, R. J., 1988: *The Roman Pottery of Kent*, Kent Archaeological Society Monograph 5, Maidstone.

PRITCHARD, F. A., 1988: 'Ornamental stonework from Roman London', *Britannia* **19**, 169–89.

RANKOV, N. B., 1982: 'Roman Britain in 1981. I: Sites explored', *Britannia* **13**, 328–95.

RCHM, 1928: *London*: Vol. 3. *Roman London*. Royal Commission on Historical Monuments, London.

RCHM, 1962: *Eburacum: Roman York*, Royal Commission on Historical Monuments, London.

REECE, R., 1980: 'Town and country, the end of Roman Britain', *Word Archaeology* **12–1**, 77–92.

REECE, R., 1987: 'The coins', in Meates, G. W. *The Roman Villa at Lullingstone, Kent, 2: The Wall Paintings and Finds*, Kent Archaeological Society Monograph 3, Maidstone.

REECE, R., 1989: 'Models of continuity', *Oxford Journal of Archaeology* 8(2), 231–6.

RHODES, M., 1986: 'The finds: discussion', in Miller *et al.* 1986, 88–95.

RHODES, M., 1987a: 'Inscriptions on leather waste from Roman London', *Britannia* **18**, 173–81.

RHODES, M., 1987b: 'Wall-paintings from Fenchurch Street, City of London', *Britannia* **18**, 169–72.

RIB: COLLINGWOOD, R. G. and WRIGHT, R. P., 1965, *The Roman Inscriptions of Britain*, Vol. I, *Inscriptions on Stone*, Oxford.

RICHARDSON, B., 1984: 'Excavation round-up 1983, Part 2', *The London Archaeologist* 4(15), 401–4.

RICHARDSON, B., 1985: 'Excavation round-up 1984, Part 2', *The London Archaeologist* 5(3), 63–7.

RICHARDSON, B., 1986: 'Pottery', in Miller *et al.* 1986, 96–139.

RICHARDSON, B., 1988: 'Excavation round-up 1987', *The London Archaeologist* 5(14), 382–7.

RICHARDSON, B., n.d.: 'The Roman pottery from Harp Lane (HL74)', Museum of London Archive Report.

RICHARDSON, B. and TYERS, P., 1984: 'North Gaulish pottery in Britain', *Britannia* **15**, 133–41.

RICHMOND, I. A., 1953: 'Three Roman writing-tablets from London', *Antiq. Journ.* **33**, 206–8.

RICHMOND, I. A. and GILLAM, J., 1951: 'The temple of Mithras at Carrawburgh', *Arch, Aeliana* 4(29), 6–92.

RIVET, A. L. F., 1964: *Town and Country in Roman Britain* (2nd edn), London.

RIVIÈRE, S. and THOMAS, A. B., 1987: 'Excavations at 94–97 Fenchurch Street and 9 Northumberland Alley', *Archaeology Today* 8(9), 13–17.

RODWELL, W., 1978: 'Relict landscapes in Essex', in Bowen, H. C. and Fowler, P. J. (eds) *Early Land Allotment*, British Archaeological Reports 48, Oxford, 89–98.

RODWELL, W., 1979: 'Iron Age and Roman salt-winning on the Essex coast', in Burnham, B. C. and Johnson, H. B. (eds) *Invasion and Response: The Case of Roman Britain*, British Archaeological Reports 73, Oxford, 133–75.

ROSKAMS, S. P. and WATSON, L., 1981: 'The Hadrianic fire of London', *The London Archaeologist* 4(3), 62–6.

ROWSOME, P., 1987: 'Roman streetlife', *Archaeology Today* 8(9), 22–5.

ROWSOME, P., 1990: '85 Queen Victoria Street (Dominant House). Excavation round-up 1989, Part 1: City of London', *The London Archaeologist* 6(6), 165–6.

ROWSOME, P. and WOOLRIDGE, K., 1989: 'Swept under the carpet: excavation and preservation at Huggin Hill', *Rescue News* 48, 3.

ROXAN, M., 1983: 'A Roman military diploma from London,' *Trans. London and Middlesex Archaeological Society* 34, 67–72.

SALWAY, P., 1981: *Roman Britain*, Oxford.

SALWAY, P., 1985: 'Geography and the growth of towns, with special reference to Britain', in Grew and Hobley 1985, 67–73.

SCHOFIELD, J. A. and LEECH, R. (eds), 1987: *Urban Archaeology in Britain*, CBA Research Report 61, London.

SHELDON, H. L., 1971: 'Excavations at Lefevre Road, Old Ford, E.3', *Trans. London and Middlesex Archaeological Society* 23(1), 42–77.

SHELDON, H. L., 1975: 'A decline in the London settlement A.D. 150–250?', *The London Archaeologist* 2(11), 279–84.

SHELDON, H. L., 1978: 'The 1972–74 excavations: their contribution to Southwark's history', in SLAEC 1978, 11–49.

SHELDON, H. L. 1981: 'London; Southwark', in Schofield, J. and Palliser, D. (eds) *Recent Archaeological Research in English Towns*, 66–9.

SHELDON, H. L. and SCHARF, L., 1978: 'A survey of Roman sites in Greater London', in Bird, J., Chapman, H. and Clark, J. (eds) *Collectanea Londiniensia, Studies in London archaeology and history presented to Ralph Merrifield*, London and Middlesex Archaeological Society Special Paper 2, 59–88.

SHELDON, H. L. and TYERS, I., 1983: 'Recent dendrochronological work in London and its implications', *The London Archaeologist* 4(13), 355–61.

SHELDON, H. L. and YULE, B., 1979: 'Excavations in Greenwich Park 1978–79', *The London Archaeologist* 3(12), 313–17.

SHEPHERD, J. D., 1986: 'The Roman features at Gateway House and Watling House, Watling Street, City of London (1954)', *Trans. London and Middlesex Archaeological Society* 37 125–44.

SHEPHERD, J. D., 1987: 'The pre-urban and Roman topography in the King Street and Cheapside areas of the City of London', *Trans. London and Middlesex Archaeological Society* 38, 11–60.

SHEPHERD, J. D., forthcoming: 'The Roman occupation in the area of Paternoster Square, City of London,' *Trans. London and Middlesex Archaeological Society*.

SLAEC 1978: *Southwark Excavations 1972–74* (J. Bird *et al.*), London and Middlesex Archaeological Society and Surrey Archaeological Society Joint Publication 1.

SLAEC 1988: *Excavations in Southwark 1973–76, Lambeth 1973–9* (P. Hinton, ed.), London and Middlesex Archaeological Society and Surrey Archaeological Society Joint Publication 3.

SMITH, R. F., 1987: *Roadside Settlements in Lowland Roman Britain*, British Archaeological Reports 157, Oxford.

STEAD, I. M. and RIGBY, V., 1989: *Verulamium, The King Harry Lane site*, London.

STRAKER, V., 1987: 'Carbonised grain', in Marsden 1987, 151–3.

TATTON-BROWN, T., 1974: 'Excavations at the Custom House site, City of London, 1973', *Trans. London and Middlesex Archaeological Society* 25, 117–219.

THOMAS, C., 1981: *Christianity in Roman Britain to AD 500*, London.

TOMLIN, R. S. O., forthcoming: 'A Roman writing tablet from the Walbrook, London', *Antiq. Journ.*

TOYNBEE, J. M. C., 1962: *Art in Roman Britain*, London.

TOYNBEE, J. M. C., 1986: *The Roman Art Treasures from the Temple of Mithras*, London and Middlesex Archaeological Society Special Paper 7.

TURNER, E. G. and SKUTSCH, O., 1960: 'A Roman writing-tablet from London', *Journ. Roman Studies* 50, 108−11.

TYERS, P. 1984: 'An assemblage of Roman ceramics from London', *The London Archaeologist* 4(14), 367−74.

TYERS, P. and VINCE, A., 1983: 'Computing the DUA pottery', *The London Archaeologist* 4(11), 299−304.

UPSON, A. and PYE, B., 1987: '79 Gracechurch Street, 1983', in Marsden 1987, 117−19.

VINCE, A., 1987: 'The study of pottery from urban excavations', in Schofield and Leech (1987) 201−13.

VINCE, A., 1990: *Saxon London*, Seaby, London.

WACHER, J. S., 1978: 'The water supply of Londinium', in Bird *et al.* 1978, 104−8.

WADDINGTON, Q., 1930: 'Recent light on London's past: a few remarks on the results of excavations in the City in the years 1924 to 1929', *Journ. British Archaeological Association* new series 36, 59−80.

WALDRON, T., 1986: 'III. The human bones from West Tenter Street', in Whytehead 1986, 101−18.

WALTHEW, C. V., 1983: 'Houses, defences and status: the towns of Roman Britain in the second half of the second century A.D.', *Oxford Journal of Archaeology* 2(2), 213−24.

WELLS, C., 1982: 'The human burials', in McWhirr, A., Viner, L. and Wells, C., *Romano-British Cemeteries at Cirencester*, Cirencester Excavations Vol. 2, Cirencester, 135−202.

WHEELER, R. E. M., 1930: *London in Roman Times*, London Museum Catalogue 3.

WHEELER, R. E. M., 1935: *London and the Saxons*, London Museum Catalogue 6.

WHIPP, D., 1980: 'Excavations at Tower Hill 1978', *Trans. London and Middlesex Archaeological Society* 31, 47−67.

WHITTAKER, C. R., 1983: 'Late Roman trade and traders', in Garnsey, P., Hopkins, K. and Whittaker, (eds) *Trade in the Ancient Economy*, London, 163−80.

WHITTAKER, C. R., 1989: 'Supplying the system: frontiers and beyond', in Barrett, J. C., Fitzpatrick, A. P. and Macinnes, L. (eds) *Barbarians and Romans in North-West Europe*, British Archaeological Reports Suppl. Ser. 471, Oxford, 64−80.

WHYTEHEAD, R., 1986: 'The excavation of an area within a Roman cemetery at West Tenter Street, London E1', *Trans. London and Middlesex Archaeological Society* 37, 23−124.

WILKES, J., 1981: 'Review of "Roman London" by P. Marsden', in *Britannia* 12, 412−16.

WILLIAMS, T. D., 1982: 'St Peter's Hill', *Popular Archaeology* 4(1), 24−30.

WILLIAMS, T. D., forthcoming: *Public Buildings in the South-west Quarter of Roman London*, The Archaeology of Roman London 3, CBA Research Report, London.

WILLIAMS, T. D., in preparation: *The Development of Roman London East of the Walbrook*, The Archaeology of Roman London 4, CBA Research Report, London.

WILMOTT, T., 1982a: 'Excavations at Queen Street, City of London, 1953 and 1960, and Roman timber-lined wells in London', *Trans. London and Middlesex Archaeological Society* 33, 1−78.

WILMOTT, T., 1982b: 'Water supply in the Roman city of London', *The London Archaeologist* 4(9), 234−42.

WILMOTT, T., 1984: 'Roman timber lined wells in the city of London: further examples', *Trans. London and Middlesex Archaeological Society* 35, 5−10.

WILMOTT, T., forthcoming: *Excavations in the Lower Walbrook Valley 1933–1960*, London and Middlesex Archaeological Society Special Paper.

YULE, B., 1982: 'A third century well group, and the later Roman settlement in Southwark', *The London Archaeologist* **4**(9), 243–9.

YULE, B., 1989: 'Excavations at Winchester Palace, Southwark', *The London Archaeologist* **6**(2), 31–9.

YULE, B. with HINTON, P., 1988: '88 Borough High Street', in SLAEC 1988, 71–81.

Index